# Money Matters

### Teens Write About
### Their Financial Fears and Strategies

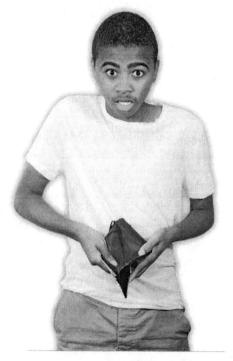

## By Youth Communication
### Edited by Virginia Vitzthum

# Money Matters

**EXECUTIVE EDITOR**
Keith Hefner

**CONTRIBUTING EDITORS**
Rachel Blustain, Sasha Chavkin, Al Desetta, Sheila Feeney,
Marie Glancy, Katia Hetter, Kendra Hurley, Philip Kay, Nora McCarthy,
Tamar Rothenberg, Autumn Spanne, Maria Luisa Tucker,
and Hope Vanderberg

**LAYOUT, DESIGN & COVER PHOTO**
Efrain Reyes, Jr.

For reprint information, please contact Youth Communication.

ISBN 978-1-938970-01-6

Third, Expanded Edition
The first edition of this book was published in 2006 under the title *Living Large: Getting Money and Spending Wisely*; the second edition was published in 2010 as *Money Matters: Teens Write About Taking Control of Their Finances*.

*Some of the stories in this edition were generously supported by a grant from NYSE Euronext Foundation.*

Printed in the United States of America

Youth Communication®
New York, New York
www.youthcomm.org

# Table of Contents

# Contents

# Contents

# Contents

# Contents

# Introduction

To teenagers, money matters. As you leave childhood behind, the ability to get and spend your own money marks your growing independence. Knowing you can buy something you want is exciting and liberating. Having some money for the first time is also a chance to mess up and learn the consequences of bad spending decisions.

Getting older means discovering more of how the adult world works—or doesn't. The gap between the richest and the poorest Americans has been growing for decades, and experts predict it will continue to grow unless politicians vote for policies like higher taxes for the rich and greater benefits for the rest of us. Young people bear the brunt of this inequality because it makes it harder to get a job and to pay for the college education you need to move up the ladder. If your parents can support you, you may not need to worry about money yet, but you will soon.

In this book, teens write about their problems handling money wisely, the lessons they've learned from managing their own income, clever ways they've found to earn and save, and their growing awareness of how our larger economic system determines their relationship to money. Many of the teens who wrote the stories in this book are in foster care or live in lower-income neighborhoods, and they write about the hard transition to economic self-sufficiency.

Xavier Reyes wasn't even living on his own yet when he found himself "trying to climb out of a deep hole" of credit card debt, from which it took him years to escape. The smartest first step to taking real control of your money is to start a bank account, as Jarel Melendez and Chantal Hylton do. But Chantal points out there are fees to beware of here, too: "A bank account is only a good thing if you know how to use it."

Several stories deal with teens' concerns about how to become financially independent. Giselle John is on a mission to save $7,000 before she turns 21 and ages out of foster care. Asia Fillmore learns not to keep bankrolling "friends" who never pay her back. (Asia's story also gives teachers an opportunity to teach colloquial as opposed to formal writing.) Whether you're trying to leave home or just want to have more money in your pocket, thrift is something most young adults will have to learn. Anita Ames writes about overcoming her prejudice against second-hand clothes. Chimore Mack turns her beloved dog into a source of income by breeding her and selling the puppies.

Yet sometimes solutions are harder to find. Shaniqua Sockwell writes of repeated frustrations in her search for a retail job. Jianxin Shi and Danielle Chambers share their experiences getting scammed by commission-only jobs that really were too good to be true. Since tuition bills loom large on a college-bound teen's financial horizon, Maria Alashola and Marci Bayer report on how to approach them, along with other college costs.

Expensive as it may be, college is important because it gives teens a better opportunity to achieve true and lasting financial independence. Marco Salazar describes his father's decades of struggle as an immigrant, and attributes much of that struggle to his lack of English skills or a college degree that is valid in the U.S. Marco's dad expects his son to receive an education and live the American dream he couldn't have.

After years of feeling "engulfed in shame" over her family's reliance on welfare, Diana Moreno makes peace with it as the support that will enable her to build a better life for herself. And when Hattie Rice is moved from her parents' rat-infested apartment to a foster care placement in a nice neighborhood, her grades climb because she sees and comprehends what she can achieve. "I'm sure that if I stay focused and succeed in school," she writes, "I can make it out of the ghetto."

Taken together, the stories in this book will help teens understand their own attitudes and assumptions about money as they prepare to become financially independent. The issues teen writers raise here can pave the way for a discussion about responsibility, values, and the way our individual spending choices fit into larger economic questions.

Names and some details have been changed in these stories: *On My Own: An Aging Out Story, A Bad Deal, How I Learned to Be Stingy,* and *I Took a Scam Job.* In older stories, dollar amounts have been adjusted for inflation or updated.

**MONEY**
**AND**
**SOCIETY**

# Don't Follow the Leader

## By Anonymous

Looking out the windows of the #3 subway train, I spot a familiar sign: Rockaway Ave. The doors open and I enter my world, my home: Brownsville, Brooklyn, one of the poorest neighborhoods in New York City.

Slowly I walk down the stairs, then push my way through the turnstile. As I step outside, I'm greeted with the smell of weed, and the sound of "Newport, come get your Newport right here" echoing through the street. Eyes gaze as I walk by. I walk fast. I'm sick of seeing those same fools drug dealing to the vulnerable or hustling on the corner.

Look straight, look ahead, and surpass the negativity. Don't get sucked up in their dimension. Keep a positive mindset, don't be one of them. Don't notice a thing.

Even after so many years, my trip home still aggravates me. It's disturbing to see the black community in this state. The thieves and drug dealers hurt each other and our neighborhood to become so-called successful. Their pride comes in knowing that they put a loaf of bread on the table. Tell me this, though: How do you feel knowing what you had to do to get it?

African-Americans have gone through so much to gain our so-called equal rights. So why are so many of us living in run-down apartments, cooped up in projects, depending on welfare, stashed up in prison and stuck in segregated communities like

Brownsville?

To find out, I talked with a sociologist at Columbia University, Sudhir Venkatesh, who spent years observing Chicago drug dealers' daily struggles to get rich or die trying. A gang member on his way to prison even gave Venkatesh detailed notes he kept about his hustling business, including how much the gang paid everyone from lookouts to leaders.

*'If you look at 100 drug dealers, 99 will make less than minimum wage. One will make a lot of money. That's the reality on the streets,' Venkatesh told me.*

People deal drugs because they believe there's tremendous opportunity to go from rags to riches, Venkatesh said. But in fact, only very few drug dealers make more than minimum wage. The gang leader Venkatesh met paid himself about $100,000 a year—or $66 an hour. (Sounds like a lot, but that's about what some experienced, unionized teachers make, when you include benefits like health care.) But the gang leader paid the three guys beneath him just a little over minimum wage and the street level dealers less than minimum wage.

"If you look at 100 drug dealers, 99 will make less than minimum wage. One will make a lot of money. That's the reality on the streets," Venkatesh told me. "It's an illusion that people have that they're going to make a lot of money. That's only the leaders driving a fancy car."

Venkatesh said that he believes teens don't choose a life of crime so much as find it difficult to get a decent job. Many African-Americans and Latinos grow up in poor neighborhoods like Brownsville where the schools usually do a poor job of preparing kids for decent jobs or college, he said. Most high-paying factory and union jobs have disappeared, so it's much harder to support a family without an education these days. And college has gotten expensive.

Racial discrimination and segregation also make it harder for minorities to start their own businesses, because many banks are unlikely to give loans to people who want to start businesses in poor neighborhoods, Venkatesh said.

Diane Hawkins-Bonaventure, deputy executive director of the nonprofit East New York Development Corporation, helps people who were on welfare get jobs. "It's always difficult for people to find jobs, but I work in the minority community, with people who've been on public assistance, and a lot—not all, but a lot—are lacking minimal education, like a GED, and have low or no marketable job skills, so it's really hard," she said.

Many of the drug dealers Venkatesh met seemed miserable standing out on the corner but couldn't see a way out. "Drug dealers are very, very scared. They don't like standing on a corner, they don't like carrying a gun. They don't know what's happening in their lives, but they're too scared to tell anybody. It's hard for them to ask for help," he said.

Poor teens get stuck on corners or in jail because we see the successful drug dealers flossing their platinum chains and spinning chromes on their Cadillacs, and we follow them. In other neighborhoods, kids see people become filthy rich by going to business school and putting on a suit.

One day I walked through Brooklyn Heights, a wealthy, mostly white neighborhood that's also in New York City. I wondered what kind of dreams the kids I know might have if they got off the train there. The neighborhood was almost picture perfect—the sidewalks weren't smothered with litter, the houses were old but not worn down, there wasn't any graffiti on the buildings.

I felt like I could breathe. I didn't have to worry about getting into an argument with any chickenheads. The streets weren't crowded, and when I spotted people they were minding their own damn business. I had no worries about my safety at all.

In that neighborhood, it's easy for kids to see the connection between getting an education and making money. In Brooklyn Heights, 60% of people over 25 have at least a college degree, and the median income is $56,000, according to 2012 U.S. Census Bureau's American Community Survey. Compare that to Brownsville, where only 20% have a college degree and the median income is about $27,000. There aren't a lot of role models in my neighborhood to show kids like me the path to success.

*The reality is that most children follow the examples of their parents and the people around them.*

The reality is that most children follow the examples of their parents and the people around them. That came home to me when I visited Norwalk, a small city in Connecticut. Riding the commuter train, I was shocked to look out the window and see enormous houses and green lawns. I usually see places like that on television, but here I was just an hour away from Manhattan. It all looked so beautiful.

When I talked to several groups of suburban teens, it struck me that all of them were expecting to go to college. For them, college wasn't an option, it was a must. They were probably so confident about college because their parents went, or their friends' parents went, and everyone around them expected them to go.

A lot of the kids in my school view college as a luxury. Everyone around us is doing so poorly that we tell ourselves, "I guess I can't break through these barriers," and we don't dare to.

When I asked Venkatesh and Hawkins-Bonaventure how they thought poor neighborhoods could change, they agreed that poor people of all ages need to come together and demand more from our government and business leaders, like a higher minimum wage and more job training.

"Advocate for change—change in schools, change in police patrols. Become more involved in what's going on in the community," Hawkins-Bonaventure said. "Go to your state representatives, city representatives, federal representatives and let them know what's needed."

They also agreed that poor teens can succeed if they get help from afterschool programs, social workers, and mentors who can show them a different path. Programs like the East New York Development Corporation already offer gang awareness and educational and recreational programs that encourage youth to stay out of trouble and in school. The large afterschool program offers help with homework and SATs, GED preparation for young adults, and a safe environment for youth after school.

Although I grew up in foster care in a hostile neighborhood, I've sought out other opportunities, like the debate team at my school and an after-school writing program. These experiences have shown me that I can look beyond the barriers I see between my dreams and me.

I know life can be really hard, and the future can seem like it's got nothing in it. It hasn't been easy trying to keep my head on in school so I can make it out. But I've used my disgust with my neighborhood and our society to become the total opposite. I wish that it could be easier for others to do the same.

---

*The author was 18 when she wrote this story. She graduated from high school and got a bachelor's degree in social work. She graduated on time, while holding several jobs during college.*

# Equal Work, Unequal Pay

By Mitzi Sanchez

Have you ever heard the phrase "equal pay for equal work"? It's something that female workers have been demanding for decades, but they're still not getting it. Men still get paid more than women in this country, and all over the world.

This is called the gender pay gap. Basically, the "gap" is the difference in what full-time workers make depending on whether they are female or male. Full-time men earn significantly more than full-time women. For example, in New York, men earn an average of about $8,000 more each year than female workers, according to a 2014 report by The American Association of University Women.

This is partly because women tend to work in lower-paid occupations, like teaching or nursing, while men tend to work in higher-paid jobs like finance or business. However, researchers find that even in the same field or even the same company, women often earn less than men in exactly the same job. For example, a 2010 study found that female professors working full-time at the University of Texas earned $120,000 per year while male professors were paid $134,000—that's $14,000 more! (The gap has narrowed since then, but female professors still, on average, are paid less.)

Some analysts say these pay differences are mostly about workers' personal choices, like the choice to have children.

Studies have shown that women start out earning about 80% of what their male counterparts make one year after college graduation; 10 years later, those same women are earning only 69% of what men of the same age earn. This might be because of the choice to become parents, which often impacts women more than men; basically, while men are getting raises and steadily climbing the career ladder, women are getting pay cuts when they re-enter the workforce after having children.

*Women get 77 cents for every dollar a man is paid in the United States.*

In fact, the American Association of University Women reviewed several studies that showed that "employers are less likely to hire mothers compared with childless women, and when employers do make [offers to mothers], they usually offer them lower salaries than they do other women. Fathers, in contrast, do not suffer a penalty compared with other men."

Many people believe that college education is the key to closing the gender pay gap, but actually, the gap between college-educated men and college-educated women is even bigger than the gap between non-college-educated men and women. Women with degrees do make more than women without college degrees, but still not as much as men who have exactly the same level of education.

| Women get... | for every $1 a man is paid in... |
| --- | --- |
| 77¢ | United States |
| 83¢ | New York |
| 65¢ | Wyoming *(the worst gender pay gap in the U.S.)* |
| 85¢ | Europe |
| 82¢ | Asia |
| 26¢ | Africa |
| 84¢ | Globally |

Sources: The American Association of University Women; International Trade Union Confederation

---

*Mitzi was 18 when she wrote this story. She is now studying business administration in college in Mexico.*

# The Rags to Riches Myth

By Marco Salazar

My father immigrated to New York from Ecuador in 1990. It was a myth in Ecuador that everyone who went to the U.S. returned to Ecuador a wealthy person. My dad knew it wasn't exactly true, and that he would have to work hard to achieve financial stability. But he also knew that even menial jobs in the U.S. paid more than most professional jobs did in Ecuador, and that there were minimum wage laws here that would guarantee he earned a certain amount.

He arrived with reasonable hopes, yet when I look at him 20 years later, I see my dad still struggling financially. I wanted to know how that happened and what he had to say about the economic recession that started in 2008 taking away any stability he had. So I interviewed him for this story.

In Ecuador, my dad studied architecture for three years. Before he'd completed his degree, my grandmother stopped paying his tuition, and he couldn't afford to complete college on his own. So when he applied for and received a visa to the U.S., he thought, "What do I have to lose?"

Arriving in New York, he moved in with his cousins in Brooklyn. He had $3,000 that his mother gave him, but to his dismay it went quickly in this expensive city. After about three weeks he was almost broke after paying for food, rent, and other expenses.

He quickly understood that pay was higher here because prices were so much higher. In fact, the ratio of expenses to pay was about the same as in Ecuador. My dad began to wonder if he should have stayed in Ecuador, but he didn't have enough money to travel back.

Although he'd studied architecture, he had to settle for a menial job here because his partially completed degree meant nothing in the U.S. He spent four months working at different factories, wishing he didn't have to work so hard. His hands had blisters at the end of the day and the pay was poor.

Eventually, a friend found him a job at an electric company; my father was glad to be working at something he was at least interested in. For the next five years he worked as an electrician's assistant, eventually gaining enough knowledge to become an electrician. He wired buildings during the hot summers and freezing winters. He wasn't happy with the workload, but he did what he had to do.

After a year working there, my dad met my mom and two years after that, I was born and he met me. My mom already had two children who lived with us, but she was working too, so for a while we were fine financially.

Then one day my dad had an argument with a supervisor, who fired him. There was a lot of racism, he explained: His supervisor was Caucasian, as were his coworkers, and my dad felt discriminated against. "They would tell me to work harder, while the others weren't told to work harder," he said.

My mother didn't make enough money at her factory job to support all of us. My dad had no choice but to work at a factory again. "I did it to support my family, not because I wanted to," he told me. After three years of working at a quilt factory, he received a call from the electric company asking him to work for them again, and he accepted.

When I was in 1st grade I barely saw my dad during the week, only at night when I watched movies with him. My father seemed happy, as was I, but that happiness soon faded. My mom died in 2000, when I was 6, and my dad was left with not only me to support, but also my half-brother and half-sister. He knew he couldn't take care of the three of us alone, so he sent my brother and sister to the Dominican Republic to live with their father.

My mom had been the one to drop me off at my babysitter's, but now I had to wake up at 4 a.m. every day to be dropped off because that's when my dad went to work. I slept there until school, and after school I went back to my babysitter's house until 7 p.m. when my dad arrived home from work.

*He had to settle for a menial job here because his partially completed degree meant nothing in the U.S.*

I was excited when my father came home. He spent as much time with me as he could. I knew my dad not working wasn't an option, but I wished he didn't have a job just so we could spend more time together.

In spite of all the hours he worked, my dad made just enough money to support us. In 2001 my uncle moved in with us, since he was having financial problems and he and my dad figured that sharing expenses wouldn't hurt either of them. But eventually my uncle moved out to start his own family, and soon after that the electrical company made cutbacks and laid off my father. He was unemployed and scared, living off odd jobs.

Luckily, a few months later he was hired by Hal's Electrical Company and after that, my stepmother (whom he married on a trip to Ecuador) and her son moved in with us. With my stepmother working and taking care of us part of the time, we were OK for about five years.

Then came the recession. With the TV full of bad news, my parents prayed all the time, asking God to help them keep their jobs. But in May 2009, my dad was laid off again, and my stepmom joined him on unemployment two months later. Now, my parents worry all the time.

Luckily there are benefits for laid-off workers, and with those benefits, we've been able to get by. My step-mom cleaned homes for a while; now she has a temporary job as a census worker on weekends, while my dad submits resumés to hundreds of employers. My parents put their faith in God, hoping he'll help them.

"It's hard to get a job nowadays; every job requires you to know English and have a college degree," my dad tells me. He understands English but speaks very little, while my step-mom doesn't speak or understand English.

"It saddens me when my children come home from school and there's nothing to eat. That's why I work hard so I can put food on the table; every little bit of money I make, I spend it on food and bills, not clothes or purses for myself," my step-mom told me in Spanish.

My father has been working hard for the past two decades to become financially stable, but he's not where he thought he would be. The recession has taken away most of what he worked for.

Even in good times, immigrants have it hard. They come to the U.S. alone and poor and often can't speak or understand English. Most come with illusions of wealth but frequently they end up returning to their native countries. Those who stay usually do so knowing they may never have financial stability, but they hope that their children will be successful. (I know my parents feel that way about me; they've always told me so, and as I get older, I'm a little nervous because I know how great their expectations are.)

In a bad economy, immigrants often feel the worst effects. "Isn't it ironic how greedy business owners are the cause of the recession, yet we're the ones suffering?" my dad said to me. "I've done what I can to support your growth and education. You're my hope, and I look forward to seeing you succeed."

*Marco was 16 when he wrote this story. He went on to attend the Massachusetts Institute of Technology.*

# A Dysfunctional Love Story

By Jan Nicole Garcia

*Capitalism: A Love Story* is a film by Michael Moore, a film-maker who is known for entertaining documentaries that are especially critical of Republican policies. He's made other famous films, such as *Bowling for Columbine*, which explored the circumstances that led to the Columbine High School massacre in 1999, and *Fahrenheit 9-11*, which looked at the presidency of George W. Bush and the war on terror. These films have won him awards as well as controversy and critics.

*Capitalism* focuses on the recession of 2008-2009 and on the problems Moore sees in our economy generally. He shows how the economy has changed over the last several decades, how many factory and assembly line workers have lost their jobs, and how wealthy people and corporations use their money and power to create an unfair system.

Early in the film, Moore says that capitalism is supposed to mean that businesses offering the best products and services will succeed and grow bigger, which sounds fair. But then he talks to laid-off employees and people being evicted from their homes to show how this system allows very big, successful businesses to bully individuals who don't have wealth or power. He even talks to priests who tell him they believe capitalism is evil.

One thing that I learned watching this film is that way back in the 1940s, President Franklin Delano Roosevelt proposed a "second bill of rights." Roosevelt suggested that everyone deserves a job with a living wage, freedom from unfair competition and monopolies, a home, medical care, education, and recreation. I think that Roosevelt's idea is fair. However, I feel disappointed knowing that 65 years later, these rights are not guaranteed in America.

Also, I felt upset when I saw scenes of families being evicted from their homes in Detroit and elsewhere. These families were unable to keep up their payments on their mortgages, so the banks and police came to evict them. The bank officials said that they needed to sell the houses to other people. But in fact, many Detroit houses are left empty because the city is so economically depressed that most people who could afford to move elsewhere have done so. The point is that the banks don't seem to care. They'd rather leave families in the streets with nothing than give them a break.

*He's pointing out that people without money or influence should join together because there is power in numbers.*

Before watching this film, I'd never thought about capitalism or what it is—it just sounded like it had to do with money. Now that I've seen the film, I agree that capitalism can be evil, if it winds up meaning the rich become richer and the poor get poorer and can't do anything about it.

On the other hand, people usually compare capitalism with communism, and I think that communism is unfair, too. Under communism, everyone has the same salary—but some people work harder than others, and I think their effort should make a difference. Capitalism is supposed to reward people for working hard, and in that way, it's a good system. We can make the system better by ensuring everyone makes a fair salary.

Sometimes it can help for workers to start their own companies—as Moore shows some people have done. At one worker-owned company he visits, assembly line workers make a very good salary: $65,000 a year. He also shows workers in Chicago joining together to protest and demand money from the company that is laying them off, and neighbors joining together to defend a family being evicted. He's pointing out that people without money or influence should join together because there is power in numbers. I like how Moore inspires us to do something about the problems he depicts.

I recommend this film to teens whether or not they're interested in the economy, because it's an unusually fun documentary. It's especially useful to teens who feel like they have too much or too little money compared to other people and want to know why.

---

*Nicole was 17 when she wrote this story. She is now in her final year at Skidmore College where she majors in neuroscience, with the goal of studying Alzheimer's disease.*

# Getting by on Crayon Money

By Diana Moreno

I grew up knowing I was on welfare. My grandma had been receiving government benefits way before my twin and I came along.

My grandma came to New York when she was 14 years old. I think her mom sent her, and that she came alone. I don't really know the history of my grandma's life, but I do know that she knew no one and spoke no English. She had nowhere to go and she was too young to work legally.

When she was 15, she had my aunt Lucy. Then she had my aunt Carmen, and then my mom, followed by Luis, Edwin, and lastly the baby, Marisol. They were all from the same man, my grandpa, who was in the picture—kind of. He contributed a few dollars here and there, but it never covered the bills or the needs of this household. My grandmother did well considering her situation: She raised six healthy children basically single-handedly.

Still, I used to be ashamed of the fact that my family was on government assistance (which can include everything from food stamps and Medicaid to cash payments). As a little kid, I was like, "So what? Who cares?" But then I got older and I became engulfed in shame. I thought that if people knew, I would be called names like "loser," "little poor girl," "bum"—you get the picture. I didn't want to be the butt of anyone's nasty jokes. And I didn't want to look at someone who knew about my situation and see the pity in their eyes.

Besides, I hated just knowing that my family had to rely on the government for help. I guess I worried about what it said about us.

In my junior high school, there were a lot of kids on welfare. But they had designer clothes with labels like Guess and Polo in spite of this. Not only did they spend their welfare money on fancy clothes, but no one admitted they lived off the government. They laughed when accused of being on welfare. You could hear them in the halls saying, "Nah, not me, son—that's b.s." Or it would be, "Are you stupid? I don't mess with that paper money."

I had no desire to act all high and mighty and lie like them. Still, their attitude affected me. I wouldn't go to the stores near the school with this "crayon money." (In those days, food stamps were brightly colored bills, not debit cards.). To buy snacks and candy I would wait to be near my neighborhood. And even in my neighborhood, I still tried to make my sister accompany me to the store so she could be the one to pay. To her, it was no big deal.

I hated going grocery shopping at the local supermarket the most. I'd have my cart full to the top, so I knew I'd be spending at least $100. After she'd passed all the food along, the cashier would ask, "How will you pay?"

There would be about 10 people behind me, all huffing and puffing, wanting to go home. And guess who they'd all be staring at? Lil' ole me. I'd feel the heat and color rise to my face as I paid with my food stamps. I'd have to count them, pull them from their books, and then wait for the cashier to re-count them, like 10 times over. I always wanted to fall through a black hole in the floor. (These days you can often use an electronic card instead, which seems much easier.)

When I would go see my mom in the Bronx, it wasn't as bad. My mom lives in the projects, and most of the people I saw buying groceries paid in food stamps. I guess I felt more comfortable because I assumed the other tenants were all on welfare.

As I got older, though, I slowly began to feel less ashamed no matter where I was. Maybe it's because I matured and didn't care that much what people thought about me anymore.

Also, when I was 14 or 15, I began to work and understand what it's like to be paying the bills and making ends meet. My grandma really needed welfare to help us live. Without government aid, we would barely be making it. Many families are in the same situation, even though they work hard and don't waste money.

Being on welfare helps us pay for really important things, like when you receive a hospital bill of $350 just for sitting in the emergency waiting room and having the nurse take your temperature and pulse. You know that Medicaid covers it and it's a big "whoosh" of relief past your lips.

It's also great that when I go to college, my family's circumstances will help me qualify for financial aid. As I've become more independent, I've begun to feel that I can change things in my life and won't always have to be on welfare. Getting financial aid for college will be a step toward making those changes.

It's not my fault that my family is on welfare. And welfare's good when plans fall through and you're in a real money bind and can't support yourself. It's good to know the government doesn't mind helping out for a while.

But living with welfare also kind of ties you down. You can get so used to it that you look at welfare as "the back up plan." I don't want to be a high school dropout who thinks she can relax and just get by on welfare. When I untangle myself from the spider's web of government benefits, I want to be able to support myself with my own earnings. But right now, I'm glad I have welfare to help me get there.

One of my biggest eye openers was when I started working as a cashier at a supermarket. I was proud to be working and making my own money for the things that I craved. But working at the store also made me see just how many people needed welfare to help them get by.

On the first of the month the supermarket was always jam packed. Everyone was shopping, with two carts full of groceries, and the checkout lines would never end. The customers just kept coming and coming, and the majority of them paid in food stamps.

It helped seeing how many other people were in the same position as my family. I stopped looking at my situation with so much shame. I still tend to feel a little weird about welfare, but just a little.

*When I untangle myself from the spider's web of welfare, I want to be able to support myself.*

Kids almost always grow up believing that they're going to be somebody someday. I have the same belief. But I know that it is possible that my life might take some unexpected turns. Anyone's life might. Some people have rich families to fall back on. Others don't. They need help, too.

I guess what I'm trying to say is that there's nothing to be ashamed of about having financial problems, or being on welfare, as long as you use it, don't abuse it. Welfare has helped me a lot, and I hope it will keep helping me until I don't need it anymore.

---

*Diana was 17 when she wrote this story. After high school she joined AmeriCorps.*

# In This Game,
# The Rich Get Richer

By Melissa A. Oliver

Imagine being suddenly thrown into adult life: You are handed a piece of paper telling you your profession, how much money you make, how big your family is—your entire destiny. Imagine having to pay all the bills and depend on no one but yourself.

That's what happened to me when I played a game called Reap and Loss with a group of about 15 teenagers at a youth program in Brooklyn last summer. The piece of paper they gave me said that I lived in a neighborhood called Nottus, was single, and had a child. I was a secretary and made $3,200 a month.

The game worked like this: First everyone had to go to the bank or check cashing place and get our money. The people from Nottus were paid in fake green money, while the people from another neighborhood—Cenbrook—were paid in fake yellow money. When we had our fake money, we had to go around the room paying rent, buying clothes, shopping for food, paying for surprise expenses (fixing a broken TV, for example), and, if there was anything left over after all that, entertainment (vacations, movies, etc.). It wasn't hard for me to pay all of my bills on time, because I had the money. My only problem was deciding how much of a certain thing I wanted to buy. I knew I could afford it.

Like me, practically everyone from Nottus had money. Many

owned land or had some type of business. But in a neighborhood called Cenbrook, people had nothing of their own. If the people there wanted to buy clothes, they had to shop at stores owned by people from Nottus who were ripping them off.

The people in Cenbrook couldn't open bank accounts simply because of where they lived. There were no banks in Cenbrook, and they didn't have cars to drive to Nottus. Even if they could get to the bank in Nottus, they didn't have enough money to keep the minimum

*Look around your town or neighborhood. How many of the people who own businesses actually live there?*

monthly balance. When they wanted to pay their bills, they went to a check cashing store where they had to pay a special fee that people with bank accounts don't get charged.

There were people in Cenbrook who couldn't pay their bills. They couldn't get loans from the bank either, because they had no credit. By the time it was all over, these people were flat broke. One girl was walking around asking, "Where's the welfare line? Where's the food stamp line?"

Another time I watched the game played, and a boy was yelling that he was naked by the end because he couldn't afford to buy clothes. "The amount of money I have isn't enough to live," another kid complained. During the discussion that followed, one girl said that she was a pizza delivery person who only made $1,000 a month, but every cent of that had to go for rent, and her landlord wouldn't give her a cheaper apartment because of the number of people in her family.

Even though I was left with $1,000 after paying all my bills and expenses, a lot of other people only had $30 to hold them over until their next paycheck—sometimes less. There were some who couldn't afford to feed their children or put clothes on their backs. One girl became homeless because she didn't have enough to pay her rent.

At the end of the game, the teens in charge asked us to hold up our money. Some people didn't have any. The people in Nottus generally had quite a bit left—and though we started out with only green money, most of us now had a lot of yellow money, too. Meanwhile, the Cenbrook residents were only left with a fraction of the yellow money they started out with. Hmm…

The point of Reap and Loss is to show how easily money can flow right out of the community where you live (in the case of these teens, "Cenbrook," or Central Brooklyn). If you don't believe it, look around your town or neighborhood. How many of the people who own businesses actually live there? Probably, many of the businesses are owned by outsiders. And what they're probably doing is taking a lot of the money that you pay them back to some other neighborhood with trees and grass, picket fences, and families with 2.5 children and a dog. A place where no one is like those of us playing Reap and Loss at the youth program. That's what "Nottus" stands for. Not us, get it?

Playing Reap and Loss made me realize that this is one reason why poor neighborhoods stay poor, while rich ones keep getting more and more money and have better things than we have. After the game was over, the teenagers who were running it (they were involved in a program called Financial Leadership for Youth) explained that one way to stop this from happening is to deposit your money in local "credit unions." While a bank is usually owned by a large corporation outside the local community, credit unions are used and operated by people who live, work, or worship in the community. At a credit union, loans go toward helping the "members" buy homes and start their own businesses, so they can take back the community that belongs to them.

*Melissa was 17 when she wrote this story. She went on to earn a master's degree in education from Brown University and became a high school teacher.*

# Movin' On Up: I Won't Let the Ghetto Hold Me Back

### By Hattie Rice

As a kid, I believed that I lived a regular life with a normal standard of living. The truth was, I was born in a homeless shelter in New Jersey and then moved on up to the East Side of Manhattan—to a rat-infested city-owned building inhabited mostly by the elderly.

Inside you had your common street pharmacist selling drugs to the elderly (they were not for arthritis) and a guy who threw his wife out the window for not buying cigarettes. The crazy part was that after she busted her ass, she ran right back upstairs to him.

One day I walked into the kitchen and saw a rat the size of a cat (I call it a crat). I'm still traumatized to this day. There were so many roaches our white wall looked black. Eventually, conditions became so bad that the floor started to cave in and the building got closed down.

By then I had figured out I was living in poverty. When my family got evicted, I had high expectations that we'd move to a more appropriate place to raise children.

My first reaction to our next apartment was, "At least it looks better and bigger—three rooms instead of two for my father, mother, brother and me." Then I took a look at my environment and realized this was the ghetto.

The block had more than enough drug dealers (it's been featured in three rappers' videos, which is definitely not a good look). This time, instead of drug dealers selling to the elderly, the elderly were the drug dealers. They were known as OGs and that's who the young up and comers got their game from.

This was also where my mom progressed from an occasional crack user to a straight-up fiend. The drugs were heavy all around us, from the corner store to the barbershop.

Our place was marked by special holes designed by the artist known as Mr. Rodent—with the assistance of his 20 or so kids. They marked our clothes, doors and even walls with their smelly signature. I woke up to a rat in the tub, one in the fish tank, or one chewing at my door to start my day. I thought the rats were normal because, being a sheltered child, I never got to see how life was on the other side of the fence. I didn't question it.

But when I was 14, I was placed in foster care, one of the best things that ever happened to me. I moved to a group home in a better neighborhood: St. Albans, Queens. This community was beautiful (although the hair braider up the block sold both weave and weed).

The streets were as clean as if somebody had licked them, and the neighbors were friendly as could be. On Halloween kids actually dressed up to receive candy. On Christmas, families decorated their front porches (hell, they had porches).

I vividly remember my brother's amazed expression when he came to visit. He had his mouth gaping wide enough to fit three pairs of Jay-Z's lips. My brother said it was the best neighborhood he'd ever seen.

Then my cousin shocked me. While everybody in my family was telling me to get out of foster care and come home, my cousin pulled me aside and said, "Look at this place and look at where we live. You would be an ass to come home."

Seeing that happy neighborhood pissed me off. How could

I have grown up thinking every home has a large population of rats when other people lived in homes where the closest thing to a rat was a pet hamster?

It was painfully obvious to me that living in private houses and enjoying larger incomes gave the people of St. Albans a more positive outlook. Parents who are well-to-do don't have four kids and only $100 for food for a whole month, so they aren't as stressed. The kids are calmer, too.

Seeing how people lived in St. Albans had a profound effect on me. I realized I was unsatisfied with my life and I progressed from being a girl

*When my brother came to visit, his mouth gaped wide enough to fit three pairs of Jay-Z's lips.*

too scared and withdrawn to go to school to being an A student determined to reach a high standard of living as an adult.

When I was little, teachers and classmates called me retarded and told me I wasn't capable of amounting to anything, so I had made it my goal to read many books and prove them wrong. Still, I'd never believed my life would be much better or different once I got to be an adult. I needed a picture of a better life to realize that my books could take me somewhere I wanted to go.

Unfortunately, six months after I came into care, I moved to another group home—one in the Bronx, positioned right next to the projects. One block above us was the Crips, and one below was the Bloods. This, of course, brought on gang violence and the shootings that sounded like fire crackers on the 4th of July.

I lived across from a park infested with rats the size of rottweilers (I call them ratweilers) and saw little kids on the street, no shoes, with just popcorn for dinner. I knew what their mom and pops were on. I know all about having to stand outside of churches, waiting and praying for a meal (and I don't even believe in God).

Every day I saw how the neighborhood affected kids' dreams. I asked one boy what he wanted to be in the future and he replied, "Nothing." I asked another, "What's your hobby?" He said, "Standing on the corner making money."

I understand why they're selling. The drug dealers are the ones with money, and if someone has a beautiful house, car and boyfriend or girlfriend, wouldn't you admire that person? The only problem is that, in the 'hood, the respected idol is a drug dealer, and people in the 'hood die over respect because they feel they have nothing else.

In theory, schools are supposed to help kids move beyond the life they know, but at my school, at least, that's not happening. Recently my guidance counselor showed me that the number of freshmen coming into my high school is staggering compared to the low number of seniors who graduate.

*I needed a picture of a better life to realize that my books could take me somewhere I wanted to go.*

Your environment molds your expectations. If you see everybody around you failing, you'll likely fail too, unless you fight like hell against it. If your dad and mom met while he was selling drugs and she was buying, it's more likely their baby will turn out to be a lookout for 5-0 than a Yale graduate.

But I believe that it's possible for me to block out everything around me and all the painful, negative things I've grown up with. I'm sure that if I stay focused and succeed in school, I can make it out of the ghetto.

Since I came into foster care, I've maintained my grades no matter what was happening in my life. And last year, when I got the chance to move to a foster home, I demanded to move to a good neighborhood and to live with a foster parent who could help me get into college.

That foster home wasn't the greatest (I've moved yet again, to a foster mom who cares as much as I do about my college education). But at least it was in a nice area downtown, a serene environment with no gunshots and no kids screaming from a beating. I felt safe walking home because I didn't hear "Yo, Shorty!" on every corner or see a bunch of broke-ass hustlers. Instead I saw businessmen talking on their cell phones.

The neighborhood inspired me and I felt like I could calm down. Nights when I didn't feel like doing my homework I'd look outside and realize that one measly homework assignment wasn't going to keep me from my dream of being successful enough to live in a nice place as an adult. Of course, I also kept a 90 average.

In school, I'd often analyze what went wrong in some of the other kids' lives. In my new neighborhood, I had a chance to see how people went right.

Walking down the street I saw role models—businesspeople on their way to work, heading into beautiful buildings. It was such a moving experience for me to walk among them, imagining myself one day working in one of those buildings or going into one of those homes, too.

---

*Hattie was 17 when she wrote this story. She later graduated from high school and went to college.*

# JOBS:
## THE
# GOOD
## THE
# BAD
## AND THE
# UGLY

# Job-Hopping to a Career

By Samantha Flowers

I'm 21 and I've already had seven interesting jobs. They include being a writer at a magazine, a tutor, a respite worker, and homeless shelter staff. Most of those jobs were internships or temporary positions that paid a stipend rather than an hourly wage—which usually means less than minimum wage.

Although I would have made more money and had more job stability if I had gotten typical teen jobs at stores or restaurants, those types of jobs are usually dead ends. I realized a while ago that I'd rather have a temporary, low-paying job that's a stepping stone to a career I'll enjoy than a part-time job that leads nowhere. So far, each job has taught me a little more about what I want to do and how to get there.

I got on this path by following my interests—in writing, working with children, and helping people—from a young age. In fact, my love for reading and writing brought me to my first internship.

I came into foster care when I was 14, and my second foster mom told me, "Samantha, you are always writing in that notebook of yours. I think the best way for you to spend your summer this year is to apply to this workshop at Represent magazine." Represent is a magazine written by and for youth in foster care. Summer interns earned a $400 stipend for six weeks and a small payment of about $15 to $50 for each completed story after that.

My foster mom helped me apply for the internship, and the week before my 16th birthday, I got in and started interning for the magazine. Writing for Represent was intimidating because I was now part of a crew in an office contributing to a publication, not just writing in my bedroom. But I realized that writing for the magazine let me advocate for other teens in foster care—and I liked that. I learned to have professional relationships with my fellow writers and my adult editors. I also learned to meet deadlines, which was hard because I love to take my time when writing.

I've stayed on at the magazine for five years now, but I realized I didn't want to just advocate from a desk and computer; I wanted to help people face-to-face. I was trying to be less shy and wanted to challenge myself by speaking up for others in person.

I earned my GED at 17, but I didn't want to go to college yet. I looked for a job where I could give back to the community and came across AmeriCorps. It's a national public service jobs program that connects people to opportunities to improve the environment, build houses for the poor, and work with children.

*I'd rather have a temporary, low-paying job that's a stepping stone to a career than a part-time job that leads nowhere.*

I especially liked the idea of working with children. Since I was 6, I've babysat younger kids—cousins and foster brothers and sisters. I was also a volunteer tutor, helping K-2nd graders with reading and writing. I like being a role model because I never had any growing up. So that spring, I applied to all the AmeriCorps programs that involved working with children.

City Year was one of those programs, for people ages 17 to 24. You have to be a U.S. citizen or legal permanent resident, and you have to commit to 11 months of full-time work. I was paid $275 weekly before taxes, which is the equivalent of about $5.50 per hour. They also provided health insurance and a stipend to put toward education. Because I was still in foster care, the pay was fine for me, but not so great for my peers who were living on their own.

The experience was much better than the pay. I tutored kindergartners and first graders starting at 8 a.m.; then I'd host workshops or do office work in the afternoon; and then after-school tutoring until 6 p.m. Some days I did community service with the whole group, and I also did some fundraising.

The City Year job ended, but the experience I got working with children and on a team helped me land a new job. I was hired as a respite worker with Mercy Drive Inc., an agency that connects families who have children with disabilities to respite workers and special needs specialists. They didn't ask for experience with special-needs kids, just that you be caring and responsible.

For that job, I went to the homes of families whose children had disabilities ranging from autism to cerebral palsy. My job was to tutor, babysit, and help the parents with their kids. I started working 30 hours a week.

I felt out of my element at first because I had never worked with children with disabilities. But as time went on, I saw beyond the disability to the child.

There were problems though. Some families wanted me to clean their houses and run errands for them, but I couldn't bill for those hours on my time sheets. They got mad when I said I wasn't a housekeeper, and my hours got cut. Some weeks I only worked 10 hours. I was getting paid $9 an hour and was told I would get promoted to $9.50 after six months but that never happened. I wasn't making enough money, so I had to quit.

I went back to Craigslist where I'd found that job, and I found another AmeriCorps position tutoring kids in K-5th grade at the YWCA. I'd pick students up from their classes and take them to an assigned class for homework help and recreation activities. I became close to my coworkers and for the first time at a job, hung out and did things with them. But because it was a temporary position like most AmeriCorps jobs, that ended in June of 2011 and I was back to job hunting again.

When I aged out of care, I didn't have a job, and I had to pay rent. I was so desperate that I fell for a scam run by a "bartending school." A manager there went on and on about all the money I could make bartending and how flexible my schedule would be—all the things I wanted to hear. He then told me that I needed to pay $199 in order to get my license.

I paid him the money thinking that I'd be trained in a popular, high-paying profession. But I looked up the "school" online and found only some reviews saying the place was a scam. I demanded my money back, and they tried to tell me I'd signed a paper that let them keep my money. I got my bank involved and filed a claim against the company. Since I had paid with my debit card, I was able to get my money back. I will never fall for a scam like that again. Make sure you do your research before you give money to anyone claiming they can help you find a job.

Finally, after nine months out of work, I came across the Young Adult Internship Program (YAIP), a New York City program for low-income young adults aged 16-24 who are not working and not in school. They partner with companies that provide internships. I was placed at a drop-in center mentoring homeless youth and assisting them with their housing and education needs. The internship only lasts 14 weeks, but I will get job-finding assistance for up to nine months after that.

*To do the jobs I want to do, helping people, I need a college degree.*

Although I'm tired of hopping from job to job, I've built up my résumé a lot over the last five years. I've learned how to be patient in a crisis from working at the homeless shelter. I know how to lead a community service project from working at the YWCA. I know how to teach life skills and hygiene to children with disabilities from working at Mercy Drive.

I went to college for a while, majoring in psychology, but then dropped out. I can see from the many jobs I have that I want to do more to help people, and to do that I really do need a college degree. I decided to go back to school and change my major from psychology to social work. I hope to make a career in social work, helping youth and advocating for change.

There are a lot of opportunities for young people—and especially youth in care—to get internships, participate in job training programs, and find work through youth employment programs. And those opportunities dry up as you get older, so my advice is to take advantage of opportunities like AmeriCorps, high school or college internships, and youth employment programs while you can.

---

*Samantha was 20 when she wrote this story. She is now working as a home health aide and was trained to be a Certified Nursing Assistant.*

If you're interested in getting work experience through a community service program like Samantha did, consider joining AmeriCorps. The national program connects people with opportunities to help others and pays a small stipend. Learn more at AmeriCorps.gov.

City Year, which partners with AmeriCorps, is open to people aged 17 to 24; workers commit to working 11 months at a school and earn some money for education. Learn more at CityYear.org.

Job Corps provides free education and training for low-income people 16 and older. Go to JobCorps.gov.

# A Bad Deal

## By Anonymous

It all started when I was homeless and sleeping on the streets. I had no money, and I felt too ashamed to go to a soup kitchen, so I would go days without eating. I had aged out of foster care and felt like I was worthless, like nobody cared about me. My plan was to hustle on a small time scale, but eventually I lost hope and just wanted food in my belly.

Then one day my friend Randy told me that he knew a guy, Jamie, with a weed service.

"I know you need a job, so we were talking," Randy said.

I was a little skeptical at first. I was nervous about things like handling a lot of money that wasn't mine, or getting caught by the police. But I'd seen Jamie at parties and he did look like he was holding money.

"How much money could I make?" I asked Randy.

"Like $150—$300 a day," he told me.

"Damn, that's a lot of money," I thought to myself. With that I could get a roof over my head and something to eat. Maybe I would finally have a purpose and not feel like dead weight.

The next time I saw Jamie it was at a bar. When I arrived, they told me to come up to the roof where the party was at. Jamie called me over and said, "Do you wanna work for me?"

I knew I was at a crossroads, but when he showed me the weed and I saw how much money I could make, there was no question in my mind. I sold my life to the devil.

"Hell yeah," I said. "I have no place to live and I need the money. I'm with it."

He sent me on my first run. It wasn't too far from where we were hanging out. Man, was I nervous. I didn't want to get run up on by the cops and I'd never dealt with weed in this quantity. But it was easier than I thought. I came back and handed him the money, and he was happy because I was so fast.

The next week I officially started working for Jamie. I would go to stops and call the customer and we would meet up on the street, in their apartment, or in their car. For the first three weeks I worked without a day off. I worked from 1 p.m. to 11 p.m. and didn't stop chilling until 3 or 4 in the morning.

It was often monotonous, but it had its moments. I got to skate all day. I followed my own schedule. And the people I met were interesting.

After two weeks of working, Jamie helped me get my own place in the neighborhood where he used to live. Jamie also got me a haircut, new kicks, and a new wardrobe, and he told me the ladies would look at me more. That gave me a confidence boost.

*Not many people my age were making the kind of money I was making. I felt like a king.*

And having a job and an apartment made me feel productive and successful. Not many people my age were making the kind of money I was making. I had everything I needed and wanted, and I was feeling like a king. I partied all the time and met celebrities. It was extravagant, and I was tired but happy. I felt so alive, like I could control anything.

When I was doing well, Jamie would tell me to keep it up. He was nice and funny, and his support helped me feel human again. Jamie gave me advice on things like stuff to buy for the crib, what to wear, and older ladies. He was there when my parents acted up. It felt good to know that someone had the heart to help me out.

But as the weeks passed, I began to realize that he only complimented me when I did what he wanted.

I t started after a restful day off, when I came over to Jamie's to start working.

"What's good, J?" I asked Jamie, like I did every morning.

"How was your day off?" he asked.

"Great. I chilled with my brother and sister on the Lower East Side," I told him.

"You shouldn't hang in the Lower," Jamie replied. His voice suddenly rose angrily and his face went beet red. "People over there know you work for me and I have beef so you can't be over there no more." A combination of liquor and rage slurred his words. "But don't listen to me if you want," he added. "If you get got then it's coming out your pocket and then you'll get fired."

I looked at him with hurt and surprise. I could have understood if he had told me to watch my back and be careful. But to tell me I'd lose my job just for going to that neighborhood? I thought he was going nuts. He was babbling and carrying on like a baby.

I just wanted him to shut up so I agreed. I bowed my head and stammered out, "You got it, J."

From that moment on, I felt like everything was out of control. Little by little he started taking over my life. Two weeks later it was where I could play sports—he said I couldn't go to the park in the Lower where I like to play ball. The guy was seriously paranoid.

I wasn't able to see my friends because almost all of them live on the Lower East Side. And since my hours and days were all screwy, it was next to impossible to see my family. Jamie was taking away the things I loved, and he was always using the job as leverage.

If I wanted to do something, I had to ask Jamie first. If he made me angry, I had to put my anger in my book bag and take it out when I got home, because anger is dangerous in this line of "work." So I kept it all in and it started to build up.

After two months on the job, I was top dog, but it came at a price. I started to notice things about Jamie I didn't like. He'd talk about people while they weren't around. He ogled females and told them the nastiest phrases. I understood then how this guy could have lots of money but no companion to share it with. It was really embarrassing to realize that this coward was trying to tell me how to run my life.

For the most part I followed his orders, because I needed the money. But I was hurt that I couldn't decide for myself about the things that mattered to me. I felt lost. I had no one to talk to *Jamie was taking away the things I loved, and he was always using the job as leverage.* because I didn't want to look soft. It almost felt like being locked up, and that was making me angry.

Still, I put up with this because I liked living on my own. I felt like the king of the world. I brought whoever I wanted into my palace. I stayed up as late as I wanted and I did whatever I wanted—in my own home, at least.

Plus, I was still confused. Just when I'd feel like killing him, he'd do something real nice and I'd feel bad. We would still party and he would lend an ear if I needed someone to talk to.

By the middle of my third month, everyone else had either been fired or quit. I was constantly worried that Jamie's mood swings would turn to me next. But I was scared to go back to the streets. Jamie knew that, and took advantage of it.

My fourth and last month was the worst. I felt like I was going to break. I was working later and later every night and getting less and less sleep every day. I was looking like hell and starting to lose my will to care. It was like he was sucking the life out of me. One day I just couldn't take it anymore.

I came to his crib to get the work and to smoke a morning

blunt when he told me to go home.

"For what?!" I asked in utter disbelief.

"I saw you with that hoody on yesterday," he said angrily.

"Are you f-ing serious, it's a hoody!" I yell at him.

"You make too much f-ing money to wear anything two times!" he screamed in my face. I just took it all in and when he finished, I picked up all my money and walked out. I felt like I was going to kill him if I stayed any longer.

"Wait! Come back and sit down," Jamie calmly called after me.

"Jamie, since you called me all kinds of names and barked on me, how about I take today off and work tomorrow?" I asked, as I tried to tuck my anger away. I figured I could plot later.

"No! You work today or you don't work at all," Jamie told me.

"I guess I don't work at all then," I said as I walked out the door.

I felt powerful and like a full man as I walked out. I didn't care anymore. Sleeping in a park in the middle of winter was a hell of a lot better than being the object of scorn and hate.

When I got home it started to hit me a little bit more. "Damn, how am I going to pay rent and how am I going to eat? Where am I going to go?" I was scared because I had nothing and no one to help me.

But I knew I had to get back to my original plan for my life—college and a legit job. Leaving Jamie behind was my first step.

---

*The author was 22 when he wrote this story. He later got a job delivering newspapers.*

# I Took a Scam Job

By Jianxin Shi

It was a hot summer during high school, and I needed a job. The employment sections of the Chinese community newspapers mostly advertised jobs at restaurants and nail salons, which required several years of experience that I didn't have. When I saw an advertisement that said no experience was necessary, I dialed the number.

"Hello!" said a woman in Mandarin. She had a cold voice.

"Hi, are you hiring?" I asked.

"Yes, we do offer jobs."

"What would I be doing?"

"That depends on your ability."

She gave me the company's address in Chinatown in Manhattan, and told me to come the following week for an interview. I thanked her and put the phone down, feeling relieved. She didn't sound very encouraging, but I thought this was the way professional people spoke.

When I arrived at the company's office, I filled out a form and then met Landy, who was supposed to interview me. She looked about 20, but her serious manner made her seem older.

Landy brought me into a small classroom where loud pop music was playing, and told me a presentation about the company would begin soon. Shortly afterward, another woman walked in and introduced herself as Tracy. "The reason that I am working in this company, Heartwealth, is because of the powerful product that this company has," she said. She told us that she used to suffer from severe acne, and as she said this, a projector displayed an image of her face covered in pimples. "I tried so many cosmetic products, but none of them worked. Some even exacerbated my condition," she said. "But after three months of using Heartwealth, my face was much better."

There were people of all ages in the room, about a dozen in total. As the presentation went on, Tracy shared other people's testimonies about Heartwealth. Their products, which were supposed to give you different health benefits, seemed impressive. But the part that excited me most came next: "We will help anyone who takes a job here to make up to $2,500-$3,000 per month," Tracy said. She explained, however, that we would work on commission. That means instead of being paid an hourly wage or monthly salary, we earned a percentage of what we were able to sell.

After talking about examples of high-earning employees, she ended the presentation with more noisy music. I still didn't know what this company expected of me, but I figured I'd probably be persuading people to buy Heartwealth powders and pills. They looked like health products I'd seen in the supermarket, so I doubted whether anyone would be willing to spend a lot of money on them.

But I was also completely entranced by the notion of earning more than my dad. I started imagining things I could buy, like a new computer, and planning how I'd continue working part-time after school started in the fall.

I also got excited about the idea of developing my speaking skills. I don't think people take me very seriously when I talk. I don't know how to make people passionate about what I'm telling them. But I imagined that by doing this job, I could learn to be mature and eloquent like Tracy and Landy and get more respect.

On my next day at Heartwealth, there was another long presentation, this time about how employees should recruit new workers to become their "team members." I did think it was unusual for a job to involve so many presentations, rather than actual work. Afterward, I was introduced to Eric, a guy not much older than me, who tried to persuade me to buy a Heartwealth product for $60. From the way he spoke, it was obvious he was giving a rehearsed speech. "You should try our product, so you will know how good it is and confidently work in this company," he said. When I told him I didn't have $60, he said, "That's just an excuse. If you really want to do well in this company, you should let go of your excuses."

*My employer claimed more and more—that our product could cure cancer, or that we could make millions of dollars a year.*

I was resolute, and finally he gave up. Though I didn't like Eric's pitch, I figured it was worth putting up with some annoyance for such great money.

I doubted some of the things I'd heard. For example, I didn't think Heartwealth was likely to dominate the U.S. market for health products within three years, as they vowed they would. But I convinced myself to ignore my doubts, because I yearned to make a lot of money and to appear as mature as the young managers I'd met working at Heartwealth.

Over the next few weeks, I spent my time on the street handing out leaflets that advertised the company's products, or doing small jobs at the company and listening to daily presentations given by the managers. Soon I began working seven days a week, from 9 a.m. to 7 p.m. Sometimes I even went out during the night on my bicycle to tape posters up on the streets.

At first I could only leaflet 400 sheets per day, but later it grew to 800. I stood at intersections handing leaflets to everyone passing by in any direction. By my fourth week at Heartwealth, work filled my day from the moment I opened my eyes to the time they closed. I was giving it everything I had so that by the end of the summer, I'd either be earning all the money I'd been promised, or I'd know for sure that those promises were impossible.

Several things raised my suspicions: When I was sent to hand out leaflets at first, I needed to have a supervisor accompanying me, even though leafleting is a job that a kindergartener could do. It seemed like the company was trying to keep an eye on us.

Once, while I was in the office, I said something to another girl, and immediately a manager stopped our conversation. "Quiet down, there are other people working," she said. They didn't want us communicating with each other.

But the most suspicious part of the company was the "lessons," or presentations, we had to attend. There was a big one every week, which usually lasted for five hours, and shorter lessons on the other days. They covered strategic leafleting and "captivating" our friends so they would buy the product or join us working in the company; there were also the lessons about the power of our product, and on the hierarchy of the company.

The lessons changed my attitude dramatically. Sometimes when I felt tired of working, I'd become energetic again after I'd had a lesson reminding me of the high commission I was working for. I especially remember the lessons taught by Mr. Bob, one of the chairmen of the company. He talked about the hard times that he had gone through as an immigrant and the steps he'd taken to become a millionaire.

*Teens should beware of any job that is based around convincing your friends to buy something.*

"Through the system we've created for you, you will become successful like me, or even better," he promised. "We never persuade people," he added, "otherwise we would be like any scam company on the market. We won't persuade you to stay with us. But if you don't want to listen to what your manager tells you, please don't waste our time, since there are plenty of other people who are willing to join us." His speeches gave me a picture of a bright future that I wanted to enjoy, and the fact that he directly confronted the doubts I was feeling made his speeches more effective, too. Why would he bring up the word "scam" if he was actually trying to trick us?

As time went on, the lessons claimed more and more—that our product could cure cancer, or that we could make millions of dollars a year. At first I didn't believe these claims at all, but eventually a voice in my head began to ask, "What if these things they say are true?" I was being brainwashed. I was spending so much time listening to something unbelievable that I was starting to believe it.

I think I was susceptible to brainwashing because I wanted to believe that this company was for real. I had always been an average student, and I was worried about my future. If I could really make a living at this company, I could stop worrying. This was such a comforting idea that I did my best to trust Landy when she told me, "As you get more teammates and your teammates get teammates, you will earn much more."

I kept working, even though doubts exploded in my head the moment I left work—and even though I wasn't earning any money. The managers assured us that we would earn money after we had been with the company a little while, gotten used to the system, and acquired more teammates. I told myself this might be true.

Eventually, I did find two customers by leafleting. One of them bought $3,000 of our product, and I earned a $300 commission. But I had become so obsessed with the question of whether or not Heartwealth was legitimate that instead of putting the $300 toward the computer I wanted, I spent $100 on Heartwealth pills that were supposed to help me gain weight. I began taking the pills and waited to see what would happen.

Meanwhile, I began talking with a couple of other young people at the company who had doubts like mine. We'd ask each other questions like:

"If this company is trustworthy, why do I feel they keep hiding something from us?"

"Why do we keep getting lessons every day?" "Is our product really capable of curing cancer?"

None of us could answer these questions, so our belief and doubts kept battling in our minds.

Finally, my fellow workers began to leave the company. One girl said her parents had called the place a scam and forbidden her to work there anymore. She told me about other people who were planning to quit, too.

My heart was suddenly filled with a sense of loss. I thought about the effort of working 10 hours a day with no rest, and about how I'd paid several hundred dollars on meals, a formal business suit, and a MetroCard. I had not earned the equivalent of what I'd spent. Maybe I'd been wrong to join this company.

Over the following week, my speed of leafleting dropped; I was no longer eager to work. Every day when I was in the office, I looked around to see who else had left. By the end of August, there were only a couple of us left, and finally my teammate decided to leave.

I was no longer working to earn money, but in hopes of finding the truth about this company for my former coworkers and myself. I tried to continue working after school began, but I'd lost all my willpower.

I gave Landy my resignation, telling her that my parents didn't want me to work there anymore, because that seemed like the easiest explanation. She reacted calmly. I'd hoped that she would give me a truthful answer about this company's true nature, but she never did. Maybe she was brainwashed herself.

Not long after, I finished using the Heartwealth products I'd bought—pills and a powder that were supposed to make me gain weight. I never gained any weight at all.

Months later, I realized that if Heartwealth was expanding around the world and curing cancer like they said they would, I should have heard about it on the news by now. I hadn't. Since then, I read online about a similar scam that spoiled the lives of millions of people in China. This type of scam is called a "pyramid scheme." One person is persuaded to join and buy a certain product, and then that person is used to attract others around him or her to join. This process is repeated, enlisting many people. It's called a "pyramid" because it requires an ever-greater number of people to keep functioning, but only the people who join early—the people at the "top" of the pyramid—have much hope of making money.

Beware a job that doesn't give you a basic wage. Scams entice you with the possibility of a tremendous amount of money, but they don't guarantee you anything. Teens should also beware of any job that is based around convincing your friends to buy something or join an organization. And stay away from any job that pressures you to make some kind of purchase up front. Legitimate jobs pay you money; they don't take money from you.

---

*Jianxin was 18 when he wrote this story.*

# Job-Hunting Tips

By Shaniqua Sockwell

After months of job hunting without any luck, I interviewed Loren Harris, director of youth employment at the Stanley M. Isaacs Neighborhood Center in Manhattan, to learn new strategies for my job search. The program trains youth and although they don't promise you a job, they help participants find employment.

When you're looking for a job, it's important to make the right impression with any potential employer. Here are some tips on what you should and shouldn't do when looking for a job:

**Appearance:** "You only get one opportunity to make a first impression. Always dress professionally," said Mr. Harris.

*DON'T:* Miniskirts and low-cut shirts are out; so are ripped jeans or dirty, faded t-shirts.

*DO:* Not every work site will expect you to dress like an executive for your interview, but it's better to err on the side of formal. That means a nice skirt or slacks and long-sleeved shirts; for men, a tie is probably a good idea. Be sure your shoes are clean and not too beat-up looking. Mr. Harris said that "young men should also be clean-shaven. No earrings, and no gaudy jewelry, one ring per hand." And for young women, "conservative earrings, no nose rings, modest makeup and jewelry." He also said that both sexes should "maintain well-groomed and conservative hairstyles." If you wear perfume or cologne, less is more.

**Speaking and Body Language:** When you go on an interview, most likely the first thing the interviewer will ask you is, "Tell me about yourself." You'd think it would be easy to answer to this question, since you know yourself better than anyone else. But surprisingly enough, many teens stutter and stumble when trying to answer this question. Remember, they're not asking what bands you like. They want to know things relevant to the workplace—are you prompt, responsible, curious?

Before the interview, search online to learn some of the questions that interviewers typically ask. Practice answers that will highlight your skills and abilities. Maintain eye contact with the interviewer, sit up straight, speak clearly, and smile. Mumbling and looking at the floor won't help.

**Attitude:** "Attitude is very important," stressed Harris, who believes you should show enthusiasm from the moment you pick up the application. "It shows the employer that you're interested in working."

*DON'T:* Come in saying "Yo, you got any applications?!" or come in rhyming to yourself or popping gum. Many employers decide whether they will even look at your application based on your dress and attitude when you pick it up.

*DO:* Smile, ask politely if they have an application, and say "Thank you" when handing it back to the receptionist.

*Show enthusiasm from the moment you pick up the application.*

**E-mail:** E-mail is a tricky thing: in person, your body language and tone of voice communicate a lot. Over e-mail, only your words speak for you—so make sure they're representing you as a serious, professional candidate for the job. When e-mailing a potential employer to ask about opportunities or follow up on an application, be polite and formal.

*DON'T:* Write professional e-mails as though you're texting one of your friends. Never use texting abbreviations.

*DO:* Begin the email with "Dear Mr. __" or "Dear Ms. __."

Clearly explain the purpose of your e-mail using complete sentences. At the end, say "Thank you for your attention" and sign off with your first and last name. If possible have someone more experienced read and critique any letter you send to a prospective employer.

**Networking:** Mr. Harris encourages teens to seek employment on their own, as well as from programs like his. "Find programs in your community that have a reputation for successfully assisting young people in finding employment." He also suggests talking to a school guidance counselor.

Harris added that young people should be open to trying many kinds of work, especially when they lack experience. "Be willing to volunteer. Attempt to build networks of friends and family members."

Resumé: It doesn't hurt to have a resumé when you're looking for work (although fast food places and clothing and retail stories usually don't require one). A resumé is a list of your work experience, education, and other skills. It helps the employer learn more about you and determine if you're right for the job. Having a resumé will also make it easier for you to fill out an application, since all the information you need will be in one place.

*DON'T:* Don't just throw everything together on your resumé.

*DO:* Set up your resumé so that it has separate sections for each category, such as Education, Experience, Achievements, and References. Also, make sure that there are no spelling or punctuation errors: if there are, the resumé will probably get tossed. It's a very good idea to ask a teacher, guidance counselor, or other trusted advisor to review your resumé before you start handing it out.

*Shaniqua was 17 when she wrote this story. She went on to attend New York City College of Technology and to work at Petland and other retail stores.*

# Dream Job or Scam?

By Danielle Chambers

Back in 2008, I had delusions about life after 18, the same delusions most teenagers have. I was going to go to college, get a job, move into my own place, and live the adult life I envisioned without any help at all from parents.

After all, amazing things were happening: A black man had a real chance of becoming president. Anything seemed possible. I was convinced I'd be able to make it on my own.

But in September of 2008 the stock market crashed and the world fell into a recession. As the economy tanked, I saw my hopes of college start to crash and burn too. Even with financial aid, I knew I'd need to work in order to afford college. I had to find a job, and it seemed to be getting harder and harder for teens like me to find one.

Finding jobs has always been difficult for teens, but after the recession hit, it became almost impossible. And when teenagers are desperate for a job, they are the perfect victims for a scam. I started noticing how many jobs were posted on the Internet and around the city promising a lot of money fast.

Lucky for me, I'd already been there and done that. I got my very first job when I was 15. The newspaper job listing said, "No experience necessary, start as soon as possible, make $3,000 to $5,000 a week to help save the planet." My eyes got wide with anticipation of the amount of money that I could be making—

and I'd be helping the earth, too!

I went to the interview. I had no resumé and no experience in anything besides school. A heavy-set, hippie-looking white woman named Kathy came out and started to tell me about all the dangers to the environment, and how their organization was trying to help stop carbon emissions and change the world.

> *I learned what the word 'commission' meant. I only got paid 30% of what people contributed.*

Kathy said my position would be as a canvasser, which meant I would be going from door to door asking people to donate to their organization. I sat there nervously as she asked, "Where are you from?" and, "How did you hear about this organization?" I was so nervous, I answered her in a whisper. Kathy went easy on me, though, and before I knew it I was hired and filling out tax forms.

Soon I, along with a dozen other fresh-faced high school and college kids, was participating in an icebreaker. "What's the name of the first movie you ever saw?" I liked it; the other kids were fun. And who knew there were so many cute boys into saving the environment?

The fun didn't last. During our first day "in the field," we each had a partner who showed us the ropes. We went from door to door and got every response imaginable: Some people cursed us out, others called the cops, and I was called a con artist right to my face. In the July heat with the rays of the sun beaming down on my skin and my hair frizzy from the humidity, I thought, "What the hell am I doing here?"

Sometimes people were nice and donated $5 or $10. That's when I learned what the word "commission" meant. I only got paid 30% of what people contributed to the organization. The first day I got no money and my partner made all the money and claimed it as his. I did the math. Thirty percent of nothing is... nothing.

The next day we got into vans and they drove us all the way

past the Bronx and into a wealthy community called Bronxville. I was in the middle of the suburbs all alone with no cell phone and no one to help me. I had no choice but to canvass, so that's what I did. But I was in a panic. In the blazing heat I prayed for some cool air. Then I looked up and clouds gathered and rain fell hard. I ran around trying to find a dry spot to dry the five-dollar bills people had donated.

I was the only black person in the entire neighborhood, and people looked at me like I was crazy. I felt so alone. My hair got wet, and my foot was bleeding from a piece of glass that got stuck in my brand new flats. I was exhausted. Later on that day a supervisor came to inspect me and see if I was doing OK. He looked at me soaking wet and upset, then got back in the car and left me out in the rain. He told me it was for a good cause. I quit the next day.

More recently, I was job hunting on the Internet and came across a website advertising jobs for teens. I filled out an application online and just 10 minutes later, I received a call to come in for an interview the next day at 7 p.m. I thought, "7 p.m.? That's really late for an interview." But I was desperate for a job, so I went.

I arrived early and saw a room filled with high school and college-aged kids trying to get some money. I was already disappointed. They wouldn't tell me what position I was applying for. It felt like a scam.

A young black man in a green shirt seemed to be in charge. He didn't look older than 25, and he played the role of the stern and serious boss. A woman in her 40s was applying for the job; she didn't seem to belong in that room with a bunch of teens. She must have really needed a job.

The stern guy in the green shirt looked at her and said, "The interview is over for you, Miss," and asked her to leave. As I sat there I saw a plain brown desk with nothing on it. One of the three men who greeted me as I walked in was sitting at the edge telling jokes and trying to make everybody come out of their shells. Then the boss man in the lime green shirt came out and finally started to explain the product we would be selling: knives.

I sat there like I was in the audience of an infomercial, hearing the oohs and ahhs of the future knife salespeople. "This is complete crap," I thought. I was so annoyed. The boss man took out a rope and showed us how a regular knife worked (not well). Then he pulled out his company knife and showed how the knife cut through the rope without any struggle. Everyone was elated. I was still skeptical.

The whole knife demonstration scene was weird enough, but I knew for sure it was a scam when they told me that each individual knife set cost $149, and that we would have to either buy our own set and then sell it, or borrow one from them. It was like they were asking me to pay to get a job.

When I left they said they would call me within 48 hours to tell me if I had got the job. They didn't call me the first day and I was relieved, but on the second day they called. I told them I wasn't interested.

*I knew for sure it was a scam when they told me that each individual knife set cost $149.*

I was alarmed about how many scams were directed toward young people just finding their way in the world. After that I became very suspicious of job offers that seem too good to be true and people who seem to want your money more than your hard work.

Many schemes target young people, but being vigilant and smart can save you from a scam. The number one sign that it's a scam job is if they ask for money up front. If anybody asks me for money, I run in the opposite direction.

Commission is trickier because it's not always a scam, but it may be false advertising. Sometimes a help-wanted ad or post will promise up to $3,000 a week, but most of the time your actual commission depends on how much you make for the company or organization. In any case, making a decent paycheck can be difficult if you're only working for commission.

I am looking for a job again, but this time I'm being careful. I want a job that will help me build a good resumé. I've learned that job-hunting doesn't just mean convincing an employer that you've got something to offer them, but deciding whether it's a place that's going to treat you fairly and help you get the skills and references you need to move on to something bigger and better.

---

*Danielle was 18 when she wrote this story. She started college at New York University.*

# Chimore Plus Eight

By Chimore T. Mack

I got my dog Prissy four years ago, when I was in foster care. At first Prissy was my foster mother's dog, but my foster mother couldn't deal with her. She decided to give Prissy to me, and we became very attached. I aged out three years ago, and taking care of Prissy has helped me deal with the loneliness of living on my own.

Prissy had two litters of puppies while I was still in care, but my foster mother sold the puppies off too quickly for me to bond with them. Prissy is a pretty black and white poodle-shih tzu mix, and people have asked me for her puppies because she's so pretty.

I feel like Prissy's mother sometimes. I make sure she eats her food, gets baths, and gets enough exercise. I wanted that special bond with Prissy's puppies too. I wanted to experience the birthing process, see them take their first steps, hear them bark for the first time. I also wanted to make the money from selling the puppies myself. I wanted to be a manager and an entrepreneur.

On April 27, 2012, I decided to let Prissy become pregnant. I decided that the lucky father would be Rey, a purebred poodle who belongs to my friend's stepmother.

I made a contract with my friend's stepmother. If Rey got Prissy pregnant, I would give her one male and one female puppy and I would keep the rest to sell. I wanted a contract to make it serious business, no games. My brother and I agreed to split the work of caring for the puppies and to split any money from selling them.

Prissy was already in heat (meaning she was ready to have sex and get pregnant). Rey came to stay at my house, and there was instant attraction. He and Prissy humped every one of the five days he was there, and then I sent Rey home.

It worked. Prissy seemed happy to be pregnant. I fed her well and took her on long walks. She got fatter and had to pee more often. Dogs' pregnancies last nine weeks, or 63 days. A week before she was due, I trimmed the hair on her belly, so the puppies could easily find her nipples to nurse.

A t 10 p.m. on June 25, Prissy started walking back and forth in the living room while I was watching 90210. She was panting and drinking a lot of water but she didn't eat anything. I turned the lights off because dogs prefer to give birth in the dark. I put a blanket and towels around her bed.

I rubbed her stomach and watched the birth by the light of my phone. Some water came out, and then as the puppies came out, a lot of blood came out too. Each puppy was the size of an apple, and they made tiny crying sounds. They were covered in gooey sacs, the placenta. As each puppy came out, Prissy bit into the sac to free the puppy, and then ate the sac. That was disgusting of her, but I had read online that dogs do that for nutrition. Each puppy had an umbilical cord that was not attached to Prissy, and I cut them close to the puppy's belly, like I had read. I felt like a doctor.

*I wanted to experience the birthing process and make money from selling the puppies.*

I thought there would be four puppies since Prissy looked small when she was pregnant. But in an hour and a half, Prissy gave birth to six girls and a boy. I named them Bailey, Flex, Jaguar, Milkshake, Cookie, Cream, and Azucar.

Bailey and Jaguar were chunkier than the others, mostly black with patches of brown. Milkshake was black and white with a heart-shaped spot. Cookie and Cream were a mixture of black and white. Azucar and Flex were all black with curly hair. They were really small.

Caring for seven puppies was exhausting—potty training them, bathing them, making sure they all got enough milk. I sometimes spent 12 hours a day taking care of them. My brother, who was living with my mother, helped out when I left the apartment.

*I learned that I shouldn't do business over social networks.*

It was very hard for Prissy to nurse because somebody was always wanting more. I fed her chicken and rice and gave her vitamins to keep her strength up.

When the puppies were two months old, I began looking for buyers. That's the age you can wean them—meaning that's when they develop teeth and start eating dog food instead of drinking their mother's milk. My brother and I posted an ad with pictures of the puppies on Facebook, Instagram, and Twitter asking $450 for each puppy. I thought I found a buyer on Facebook, an acquaintance, but it went wrong when this girl didn't like the price, which led to an argument on my public Wall and then a broken friendship.

I then told anyone who was interested to private-message me since I wasn't trying to go through any public fiascos on Facebook. I wanted people to take me seriously as a business-woman. I tried to persuade buyers by posting pictures of the puppies and talking up the good points of poodles and shih tzus.

I learned that I shouldn't do business over social networks. I should do it via e-mail to keep it more professional. Even though I'd asked people to private-message me, they still posted public comments. People posted that I was overcharging, and that scared away some customers.

The first two to go were Bailey and Milkshake, to my friend's stepmother, the owner of Rey, their father. I had found three potential buyers. One stood me up, but the other two were committed and they ended up buying Jaguar, Azucar, Cookie, and Cream.

I lowered the $450 price for everyone because people were complaining about the prices. For the four I did sell, I received altogether almost $1,500, which I split with my brother. I used the money to buy food for Prissy and me and pay my rent. I still missed the puppies even though it was a lot of work.

I was glad when Bailey and Milkshake left, but also sad because I'd built up an attachment to them. I couldn't help it. It was also hard when the other puppies went to their new homes. I decided to keep Flex so Prissy could have company when I'm not home.

I would like to breed Prissy again. I had fun taking care of the seven puppies. I sometimes call myself a grandma because I still ask the new owners how the pups are doing.

The experience has made me think about my own future as a mother. I used to want seven kids, but now I want only five. I realize it's a lot of work just having puppies, much less kids.

My, Prissy's, and Flex's relationship is like a roller coaster. Flex is good on some days but very frustrating when she doesn't listen. Sometimes she cries if I don't pick her up, like a toddler crying for something to eat. It's more work with two dogs, but Prissy has become calmer now that Flex is with her 24/7.

I would like to go through it again within the next two years. It was a good and surreal experience, and I got some practice running a business. Taking care of the puppies as well as the mother dog took a lot of patience, but I learned that I can handle it.

---

*Chimore is working toward her college degree and taking care of Prissy and Flex.*

BANKING
BASICS

# I Keep My Money in the Bank

By Jarel Melendez

Last summer, I got a job at the Children's Aid Society in New York. When I got my first paycheck, my supervisor, Mrs. Jean Marie DeVeaux, asked me if I had a savings account.

"I don't have any money! Why would I need a savings account?" I laughed. I thought only rich people used banks. I had never been in a bank or known anyone in my family to use one. My grandmother, who I live with, pays all her bills with money orders.

Mrs. DeVeaux told me it was important to start saving now to plan for my future. She took me to Apple Bank, where she said I could cash my $250 paycheck and not have to pay a fee like I would at a check cashing place. I was a little nervous and had a million questions in my head: Is a bank card like a credit card? What is the purpose of having a savings account? When you put money in a savings account, where does it go?

Mrs. DeVeaux had her own account at Apple Bank and introduced me to the manager, saying, "Jarel is here to cash his check. He also wants to know how to open an account and join our Apple family." She let out a little chuckle.

He said, "Oh, how nice! Sure! Let's cash that check really quick." He pointed out the people at different bank stations, who are called tellers, and told me to come back to him when I finished cashing my check with one of them.

The bank teller was really cool and down to earth. After she gave me my money, the manager and I sat down and talked bank business. He explained that I could open up an account with as little as $100, and that the longer I left money in my savings account, the more my money would grow.

Here's how it works: The bank takes in and uses your money, but actually pays you for this in the form of "interest." That means your money is working for you to make more money! He also explained that opening a savings account would help me establish credit, in case I ever want to buy a home or car

*Since my money goes right into my account, I don't spend it on things I don't need.*

or get a credit card. ("Establishing credit" means building your record as a person who is likely to pay back their debts responsibly.) Best of all, having an account would allow me to cash all of my checks there without ever having to pay a fee, like you have to at the check cashing place.

Then the manager told me that I needed a state ID, my school ID, and my most recent report card to open a student account. I didn't have any of those things. "When you have those ready, come in and we will open up this savings account," he said.

It took me a month, but I finally got a state ID and all the other things he asked for. When I went back the manager remembered me right away. He even remembered what outfit I had on, which completely blew me away.

He copied the documents I'd brought in, and I signed a lot of papers. Then he gave me a booklet explaining all the bank's policies and rules. "Your ATM card should be arriving at your house shortly," he said.

I left excited. I looked forward to receiving my ATM card, which would allow me to take cash out of my account at almost any ATM machine (although it costs extra if you use a different bank's machine). Actually, the ATM card I got was also a debit card—meaning I can swipe it at a store to pay for things, the same way I'd use a credit card. But unlike a credit card, the debit card takes money straight from my account. (With a credit card, the credit card company pays the charge and you pay back the credit card company with a monthly bill.)

In time, I also opened up a checking account, which lets you write checks to other people. When they cash the checks, the money comes out of your account. Later, I got a job at a clothing store and was able to get something called "direct deposit." Instead of giving me a paycheck, my employer automatically put the money in my checking account, which saved me a trip to the bank.

Checking accounts don't earn any interest, so it's good to have a savings account too. (Keep in mind, though, that interest rates tend to go up and down; so will the earnings on your savings account.) My checking account is for everyday use and my savings account is for long-term savings.

My future plans include building a house, and for that I will need excellent credit. When it comes time for me to get a credit card, the banks will be able to look at my accounts and see I've been responsible in handling my money. Also, saving money is important because I want to make sure I have something to fall back on in case I get fired from my job or have an unexpected expense.

I deal with my money very differently these days. Before, if I had a check in my hand, I'd cash it and spend it all on clothes, shoes, and DVDs. Now, since my money goes right into my account, I don't spend it on things I don't need.

I don't know how much I'm saving by not using a check cashing place, but I know it's a lot because I don't have to pay fees to cash my checks or get money orders. And I don't have to stand in those lines, either.

*Jarel was 21 when he wrote this story. He later worked as an AmeriCorps volunteer, graduated from college, and got a job in social services.*

# A Guide to Drama-Free Banking

By Chantal Hylton

My printer had run out of ink and the replacement cartridges could only be bought online. Simple enough. But unfortunately my grandmother didn't want her credit card information "all over the Internet." Her solution was for me to buy a whole new printer. As I stood outside Staples with my new industrial-looking machine, I made up my mind. I needed my own bank account so this kind of ridiculousness wouldn't happen again.

Soon after, I visited a Chase Bank branch and learned about a student checking account that I qualified for. I decided to open one. All I needed was my Social Security card, one other form of identification, and $20 to start the account. They told me I didn't need my parents' permission if I was 17 or older. Even better, there was no minimum balance. (A balance is the amount of money in your bank account. The minimum balance is a set dollar amount that the bank says you must have in that account at all times or you may have to pay a fee.)

Having a bank account makes me feel secure about stepping into adulthood. If used correctly, a bank account can actually save you a lot of unnecessary costs. Unfortunately, a lot of people don't have them.

I learned recently that there are high costs associated with not having a bank account. For example, if you have a check to cash, you pay a check-cashing fee. If you have a bill to pay, you pay a fee to get a money order. And for adults without bank accounts, it's difficult to get a low-interest loan if they need it. That means they face big obstacles when they try to buy a home or start a business.

**W**ith a bank account, cashing and writing checks is free, and you're much more likely to get a loan if you need one. But people can get scared off because banks often have unpredictable fees, like "overdraft" fees.

You "overdraw" your account when you pay for something with a check or debit card but don't actually have enough money in your account to cover it. Say you pay for a $5 sandwich with your debit card, but you only have $4 in your account. Instead of saying "funds not available," the bank will cover you for that extra dollar, but then typically charge you a $35 fee for the transaction. Your $5 purchase could end up costing you $40. Do that more than once, and you might be scared out of ever having a bank account again.

But it doesn't have to be that way. The key is to do your homework first, and shop around before you open any account. When you go to a bank, ask what they have in the way of simple, no- or low-fee accounts. (They won't always advertise these, so you need to inquire.)

*Having a bank account makes me feel secure about stepping into adulthood.*

Student accounts are often ideal; otherwise, look for something with a low starting deposit and low minimum balance. Also be sure to find out whether there's a monthly fee or a fee for making more than a certain number of withdrawals each month. (A withdrawal means taking money out of your account, either by writing a check, getting cash at an ATM, or using a debit card to purchase something.)

Finally, make sure you won't get stuck with overdraft fees. The law requires banks to ask you if you want that "overdraft protection" that turns your $5 sandwich into a $40 purchase. They'll try to make it sound like a good idea, but just say no. You might get embarrassed if you try to spend more than you have, but at least you won't be in debt.

A bank account is only a good thing if you know how to use it. Understanding fees up front will help you make an informed decision and avoid getting blindsided if you do decide to open an account. This might all seem far-off for many teens, but if your age is in the double-digits, you're pretty close to being on your own. Soon enough, you will have a job and need to learn how to manage your money—no ifs, ands, or buts.

Believe me, just saving your cash under the mattress or in a dresser drawer isn't wise. Just ask my aunt, who saved hundreds of dollars in a drawer full of scarves. When her daughter helped her remodel the house, lots of stuff got thrown out, including her cash!

---

*Chantal was 17 when she wrote this story. She graduated from SUNY Buffalo, where she majored in social science and is now working towards a masters degree in special education.*

# My Credit Card Gave Me False Security

By Zhanna Raymond

I got a credit card when I was 19 because I thought it would make me feel better about myself. All the adults I knew had credit cards. Most of my coworkers at Berkeley College used theirs as their main form of payment; one got approved for a card with a $10,000 limit. And that made these people seem as if they were freer, with more possibilities. Before getting a credit card, what I could buy was limited to the amount of cash in my pocket.

I was turned down for a credit card by a couple of banks because I had no credit at all—I had never taken out a loan or bought anything on layaway. Banks want evidence that you can pay back money on time. But I was finally approved for a card from Citibank with a credit limit of $1,800 and no interest for the first nine months. This meant that even if I didn't pay the full amount at the end of each month, I wouldn't pay interest—for nine months.

The card also had a point system with rewards like gift cards, laptops, and cash. The more I spent with my card, the more points I'd accumulate for a reward. Shopping at certain pricier stores would get me double points. Reading the fine print is important. Some credit cards charge annual fees just for the privilege of getting points.

I went a little crazy. I bought things that I otherwise would have saved up for. I charged a couple of trips to the Caribbean—and the souvenirs too. I purchased clothes and went to expensive restaurants and used the excuse that I'd be able to make partial payments. Having clothes and gadgets that were out of my reach before made me feel richer and more powerful. Whatever I wanted I could have.

About a year after I got my Citibank credit card, I was shopping at JCPenney one day. I didn't shop there often, but whenever I did, the cashier would always mention that I'd get 20% off my entire purchase if I signed up for a card. I was buying a lot that day and applied to get that discount. In about four months I used it enough to earn a platinum card, which meant that I'd spent over $1,000. It also meant I earned more coupons—which enticed me to shop there even more.

When I got the JCPenney card, I had just started accruing interest on my Citibank card, and the JCPenney card charged interest right away. The excitement of owning a credit card faded after the interest charges kicked in. They faded even more when I needed to juggle two payments. I had understood before that this was borrowed money, but without the interest there was no penalty for using my credit card.

*The excitement of owning a credit card faded after the interest charges kicked in.*

But now there were penalties. On top of the interest itself are extra fees, and if you skip a payment, the interest rate goes up, so you owe even more. I remembered the idea had been to build credit, not build debt. At this point I owed about $1,000 on my Citibank card, and could pay back about $300 monthly. Even though I paid it back, I was still using my card and being charged $25-$35 in interest each month. I also had to make payments on my JCPenney card, although I didn't use it as often.

realized I wanted to be smarter about spending and not go into debt because of material things. Now, my immediate goal is to finish paying down both credit card balances. I'm almost there. Once I clear that debt away, I'd like to save at least $100 each month.

Now I check how much money I actually have in my bank account before I shop. If I'm looking for something specific, I go to the mall with the idea that I'm spending $25 on a blazer, and a blazer only. If I can't pay for an item with the cash I have on hand, I think twice about whether or not I really need it.

Shopping online also helped me to curb my spending. I have more control online. I can just look at specific things that are in my size and my price range, and not get carried away with something beautiful in a store. Also, the wait for shipping holds a bit of suspense and excitement.

So far I've been really diligent about making payments for both cards that are on time and more than the minimum required. Whenever I have enough additional money to put toward my credit card bill, I pay even if it's not yet due. Ideally, when I use my credit card in the future, I will try to pay my entire balance by the end of the month. That way, I won't have to pay any interest.

*On top of the interest itself are extra fees, and if you skip a payment, the interest rate goes up, so you owe even more.*

I don't plan on applying for any more credit cards in the near future, or asking for a credit increase. I feel as though the two I have now will help me to establish credit, and I never want my spending to get out of control. I'm glad that if I need a pair of shoes I can buy them. Recently my brother and sister (ages 7 and 8) outgrew their winter coats, so I was glad I could buy them new ones. Some things are worth the interest if you really don't have the money out-of-pocket and the purchase is important. Just try to pay at least the minimum payment every month.

There's a false sense of power that comes with credit cards, but in the end, clothes wear out, and the bill is still there. There will probably always be some new shoes or gadget or pair of jeans that I admire, but part of being an adult is sacrificing some of what you want right now in order to meet other goals.

*Zhanna is now in her final year at Hunter College.*

# Budgeting with Mint.com

Mint.com is a great budgeting tool. Here's how it works: I put in the balances of my bank accounts as well as my list of monthly expenses. Now that usually looks like this:

- $104: Metrocard
- $150: food (groceries, restaurant, fast food)
- $160: cell phone
- $200: JCPenney bill
- $200: Citibank bill
- $500: housing fee for dorms (varies per semester & month)

Mint.com lets me view all my spending, track it on charts, and see how much of my money I actually spend on shopping or going out to eat. The Mint app sends me alerts when I'm nearing my budget limit for fast food or clothes. In addition to budgeting, I'm also able to create goals for myself, like saving up for a vacation or taking a summer class that isn't covered by financial aid.

Mint.com sometimes sets too-lofty aspirations for my finances. I don't have as much money saved as Mint tells me I should have, and I don't use cash as often as it recommends. So I still also use pen and paper budgeting, when I want my own realistic layout of what my spending will look like for that particular month.

# Learning What 'Overdraft' Means—the Hard Way

By Chimore Mack

I was 17½ when I graduated from high school and I had plans to head to college in New Hampshire. Over the summer, I got a job and it felt great to be working. I could pay my tuition and I had some money in my pocket.

I wanted to save my money to pay for things like clothes and transportation to get back to New York to see my family. So I went to Citizens Bank to open an account. With a bank account, I thought I'd have a safe place for my money and wouldn't be as tempted to spend it.

I didn't know anything about having a bank account. The representative at Citizens didn't really break it down for me. She just told me to be careful about going into overdraft.

I didn't know what she was talking about; I just thought that having a bank account meant I could have a debit card. To me, a debit card represented freedom and independence. It would show I could be responsible without relying on someone else.

I completed the application to get both a checking and a savings account. I ordered a checkbook and paid extra for cute Mickey Mouse checks. They also gave me a green debit card. I was ecstatic that it was green, because green is one of my favorite colors, and it represents money.

The problem was, I didn't understand that every time I swiped the debit card to pay for something, the money came right out of my checking account. I didn't understand that if there wasn't enough money in my account to cover my purchases, the account would go into overdraft, meaning I'd owe that money to the bank plus penalty fees.

I didn't understand that if I spent more money than was in my account (also known as having a negative balance), I'd have to pay it off. If I didn't, the bank would report me to a collection agency. I only thought about using the card to get points and rewards (every time I bought something, I'd get points toward free prizes).

After I received the debit card, I let my mother know about it. She wanted me to be independent, but she warned me to be careful.

"Chimore, you need to be practical with your money. Because if you don't you will have problems for years," my mom explained to me.

"Yeah, I know already," I replied, not wanting to hear a lecture from her.

"For example, you shouldn't have bought that Mickey Mouse checkbook, you should've got plain checks for free."

"Mom, it's my money and I can do what I want with it. If I get a negative balance or waste my money on nonsense, let it affect me," I sassed at her.

*I didn't understand that every time I swiped the debit card to pay for something, the money came out of my checking account.*

I didn't want my mother to say anything else on the matter, so I changed the subject. I wanted to be independent and I wanted her to know that I wasn't a little girl anymore; I could handle my business on my own. The truth was I didn't actually know how to handle my business, but I didn't realize that until it was too late.

Since I hadn't looked at the monthly statement the bank sent me, I didn't notice that almost every time I used my debit card, they added a fee. Every time I used an ATM at a store, I'd get a $1-$3 fee. When I withdrew money from a bank other than my own, they'd charge another fee—sometimes as much as $5.

After two months, my mother's prophecy came true. I had a negative balance of $98. I couldn't believe it. I was pissed off, wondering how it had happened.

I finally looked over my monthly bank statement. Between all the fees, my Mickey Mouse checkbook, and the money I spent on transportation, my account had gone into overdraft. It hadn't taken long at all. I didn't keep on top of my balance like I was supposed to, so those fees kept crawling in on my account like a snake eating up its prey.

I called one of the representatives from Citizens Bank and got another shock: My account had been closed because I hadn't paid off the negative balance. I didn't get any warning call. If they sent me a letter, I never got it. To make matters worse, the bank had already reported me to a collection agency.

Things weren't going well for me. I didn't have a job anymore, so trying to pay off the bill was difficult. I looked for a job but I couldn't find anything.

*To make matters worse, the bank had already reported me to a collection agency.*

The collection agency offered me a payment plan to pay off my debt little by little. But since I wasn't working, this didn't help much. Since I was in foster care, I had a little bit of income from my foster care allowance and stipend—$100 a month. That was for clothes, hygienic items such as soap and deodorant, and other miscellaneous things.

But I really wanted to pay off my debt, so I started tutoring and babysitting. I was able to start paying $10 a month to the collection agency, but even that was difficult. I needed to start saving money for transportation to get back and forth to school.

I told my foster mother that she should increase my allowance because the money she was giving me every month wasn't enough. I thought that was fair, since I always do my chores. She agreed, and this helped motivate me to make money my responsibility.

Little by little, I paid off the debt, and I have learned my lesson about bank accounts and debit cards. Yes, it's your own money and you can do what you want with it. But I also have learned that being independent means being able to manage your money carefully and not buy a lot of things that you don't need. It also means educating yourself about the way banks work and knowing what you're getting into before you open an account.

I still keep my green debit card in a special box to remind me about being responsible with my money and not spending it on foolish things.

## What to Know Before Opening an Account

When I opened my first bank account, I didn't ask a lot of questions and I ended up in a big financial mess. You need to know what kind of bank is best for you and understand the pros and cons of opening an account at that bank. Look for:

• A low-fee or no-fee checking account. A fee is an amount of money a bank charges you for things like using another bank's ATM, or overdrafting (spending more than you have in your account).

• An account with no minimum balance. Some banks charge fees if the money in your account, or balance, drops below a certain amount.

• A bank that has its own ATMs, including ATMs near where you live and work and/or go to school, so you won't end up using other banks' or businesses' ATMs. You can use your own bank's ATM for free, but usually pay a fee for each withdrawal from any other bank or store.

And just because you talk to a bank representative about opening an account doesn't mean you have to open one at that particular bank. Here are some questions you should ask before deciding on a bank:

• What types of bank accounts do you have, and what fees do you charge?

• What is the minimum amount of money (minimum balance) I have to keep in my bank account? What happens if my balance goes below that? What are the penalty fees?

• What is the fee if I use another bank's ATM?

• How do I know if my account has a negative balance? What are the overdraft fees if I have a negative balance?

• How can I transfer money between my checking and savings accounts? Is there a limit to how many times I can transfer money between accounts each month?

---

*Chimore is working toward her college degree.*

# We Don't Save for a Rainy Day

By Natalie Neptune

Many adults think teenagers are careless with money. They criticize us for spending money on expensive name-brand clothes, on music, and on other items they consider unnecessary.

Are all teenagers so irresponsible? I didn't think so. I thought plenty of people my age would be saving money for college or other important things. So I set out to prove that there are responsible teenagers.

I ended up a little disappointed. When I interviewed teens at a local mall, I found one who had spent $440 on music. Another 16-year-old admitted to spending most of her money on weed and alcohol for parties.

Karla, 14, said she manages to save a dollar or two whenever she can. But mostly she spends her money shopping for dresses, nail polish, music, and other things that don't seem worth it to me.

She receives a weekly allowance of $15, plus an additional $4 on school days for lunch. She also earns $30 every time she baby-sits for her cousins. But she said she wishes she had an ATM in her house so that she'd have the money to buy anything she sees and likes.

She has no goals for saving. Perhaps that's why she wastes money—like she did when she spent $37 on a tattoo she'll have to hide from her mother. I'd expected that a teen with so many sources of income would think strategically about her money. But Karla spends whatever she gets and still isn't satisfied with what she's able to buy. She said if she had more money, she'd go shopping every day.

On the whole, though, the teens I talked to who had jobs and were working hard seemed to be the most careful with their money. Meanwhile, those who had no jobs talked about spending money as if it grew on trees. Among the teenagers I interviewed, six of the 10 said they practice some form of saving. Some store their cash around the house; others save it in a bank account.

*The teens I talked to who had jobs seemed to be the most careful with their money.*

Even among these teens, there weren't many who seemed really careful about their saving. One who did was Tanya, 17, who is in foster care and lives in a group home. She is putting aside money for when she moves out to live on her own. "Knowing that I'm going out of the group home and I'll be on my own" motivates her to save, Tanya said.

Aphrodite, 18, said she saves because she's afraid of failure. "You must have something to grab on to when you need it," she said.

When I started this article, I was on a mission to prove to adults and to myself that there are teens who are responsible with money. Now, I can say it's true that some teens are very responsible. There just aren't as many as I had thought.

---

*Natalie was 16 when she wrote this story. She went on to graduate from Vanderbilt University and became a nurse.*

# Saving Money Makes Me Feel Safe

By Damaris Medina

There was a psychological study done back in the '60s by a researcher named Walter Mischel that looked at self-control in children. He sat a kid at a table with a cookie (or marshmallow or pretzel) and told her that he had to leave the room. He said that she could eat the cookie while he was gone. But if she waited until he came back, she'd get an even bigger cookie.

All of the kids in the study tried to hold off on eating the cookie until Dr. Mischel returned. But many of them didn't have the self-control to wait. And guess what? Those kids who waited ended up being more successful in life.

I'm pretty sure I would have been one of the kids who waited for the bigger cookie. I've always had a lot of self-control with spending money, even when I was little. I don't go on shopping sprees when I come across money. Instead I put it right into my bank account and hold on to it until something more worthy or necessary comes along.

I'm thrifty, too—there is nothing wrong with shopping for sales! It's not like I walk around like a bum with cheap things. I just know how to find bargains.

When I grow up I want to be rich, which means the best thing for me to do right now is to save the little money I get. I'd much rather watch my cash grow than spend it on stuff that's not going to seem important to me tomorrow. I always feel like I need to save my money because I never know when something more important is going to come along. I don't want to be stuck and not have any money to back me up.

I was the poorest of the poor when I was younger, and I mean dirt poor. There were days when the only food was maybe a small package of oatmeal in the roach-infested cabinet, and that was it. When Mom got her food stamps, it was like a miracle. But sometimes the food only lasted for two days.

I've been in foster care since my mom died six years ago, and I still consider myself poor. Now, though, it's because the money I get from foster care and working goes straight in the bank and I consider it off limits most of the time. I save because I don't want to be poor ever again. I want to be financially prepared in the future so I can avoid those desperate experiences of my childhood.

Sometimes, though, I wonder if I take things too far. When I notice that my money is going low, I feel like I have no power and it makes me feel very limited. You need money, especially if you're a college student like I am. Although I have scholarships and grants to help cover my school expenses, I still have to take out thousands of dollars in loans every year to pay my tuition.

People often think my saving habits are strange; they can't understand why I work so hard to save. Sometimes they make me feel like there's something wrong with me. Why do I feel such a strong need to save my money when other people just spend, spend, spend? I wanted to understand this habit better, so I interviewed Professor Eric Schoenberg, who teaches at the Columbia University Business School and studies the psychology of money. Schoenberg supported my feeling that saving money does provide a sense of safety and security, yet there could be other factors involved.

According to Schoenberg, there are two main things that

drive people to save money. One is called goal-directed saving, which is saving up money for a particular purpose: a house, a car, even a new phone.

The other is called precautionary saving, which means that someone saves because they have concerns about being financially secure in the future. That's the kind of saver I am. I'm not always saving up for som ething specific; I just want to make sure I have enough money for when I really need it.

Professor Schoenberg also believes some people save money because they feel social pressure to save—if they've seen their families and friends saving, they feel like they should be, too. It also means those who have not seen other people with the habit of saving may be less likely to become savers.

Self-control plays a role in our spending habits, too. Part of that, said Schoenberg, is genetic. But another part of it is life experience. He said kids who grow up poor or in foster care may have a harder time saving because it's harder to imagine the future. If you've been separated from parents and other family or experienced a lot of difficulties, it's hard to visualize things being better. You have less confidence that things will go according to your plan.

*Being thrifty and cautious now is going to help me reach my goal to live comfortably without having to worry.*

In that situation, it makes perfect sense, said Schoenberg, why people might live for the present and give in to temptation, not knowing when an opportunity will come again.

Remember the cookie experiment? It turns out that the kids from middle-class and wealthy families were able to resist eating the cookie longer than poor kids. Why? Schoenberg thinks it has something to do, again, with being able to visualize the future (having faith that you'll be rewarded with a bigger cookie). It's hard to plan and save for something that seems far away, like college, if some basic need isn't being met, or if you've had bad experiences that make it hard to imagine a brighter future. So you live for the moment.

According to everything Schoenberg said, I should have turned out to be a spender. But somehow, I didn't. Schoenberg said something about life experience that helped explain why I hold onto my money.

He compared it to being the child of an alcoholic. Some children of alcoholics become alcoholics themselves, but others avoid alcohol altogether because they can visualize the consequences—they've seen bad things happen to their parents. It can work the same way with money: If you've seen the adults around you struggling to get by, or spending themselves into debt, you can visualize that happening to you and that makes you want to do something different. As Schoenberg said, "You know the negative experiences you want to avoid."

Having money makes me feel safe. I want to be able to pay off my college debts. I know that being thrifty and cautious about how I spend money now is going to help me reach my goal to live comfortably without having to worry about the future.

So is saving money a habit that could be developed over time? Schoenberg said if you're a spender, developing the habit of saving involves making it a deep emotional experience. You have to first visualize a future the way you would like it to be. Then, you have to think realistically about how much money you'll need to get there.

"You have to make people realize what the consequences of their actions could be," he said. "I am convinced that forcing people to think about the possibilities is the single most effective technique to change behavior."

---

*Damaris was 20 when she wrote this story. She went to Hartwick College in Syracuse, NY.*

# I Shopped Until I Dropped... Into Credit Card Debt

By Xavier Reyes

My debt problems started when I went to college and got my first credit card. I was 17 years old. Like every other college freshman, I was bombarded with credit card applications in the mail. Since I was working as a youth advocate and as a waiter, I figured that if I got a credit card and used it to buy the things I needed, I would be able to pay the bills when they arrived.

So I applied, not for one credit card, but for three. As luck would have it, I got approved for all of them. I was very happy with myself and felt more like an adult.

As soon as my credit cards arrived in the mail, I headed off to shop. At that time I was going through an Adidas phase. With my credit card I bought a whole lot of Adidas stuff, as well as music and video games, and I started eating out a lot. It was amazing. I didn't have to have the money to buy these things, but with my credit cards whatever I wanted was mine.

Each card had a credit limit of $700, which meant I could spend up to $700 with each card. I managed to reach this limit—or "max out" the cards—fairly quickly. When the bills came in I paid the minimum amount that was due, which wasn't more than $25 per card.

I thought I was doing the right thing as long as I paid the

minimum amount due and paid it on time each month. And, because I had started to get used to using the credit cards so much, as soon as I would get some credit available on the cards, I would immediately use it to buy something else. I enjoyed this. Being able to buy anything I wanted was a luxury for me and I took advantage of it.

But soon even the minimum amount I had to pay—the $25—started becoming difficult. In addition to my credit card bills, I had other bills. I had to buy books for school and pay for my transportation and food. I bought my first semester books with my credit cards, but I didn't have enough credit to cover my second semester books. I also had a monthly cell phone bill that was not cheap. At night, I loved going out and partying. (Do you know how easy it is to spend $100 a night in New York City?)

While it always seemed that I had money, I was never able to hold onto it for long. I was making about $533 every two weeks at my part-time day job, and another $266 from my weekend job. But I wasn't saving anything. I was too busy spending.

I also started to notice that paying the minimum balance was hardly putting a dent in what I owed the credit card companies. This is how credit card companies earn money: Say you owe $400. Even if you pay the minimum amount due and don't use the credit card to buy anything else, the next month you will owe more, because they charge you interest on what you still owe. Believe it or not, it might not be long before the $400 you spent has turned into $800.

My own bills skyrocketed. Soon I owed $2,400 to the credit card companies. I felt I couldn't handle the bills, like I was trying to climb out of a deep hole, but the more I tried the further I fell.

For a while, I paid what I could afford. But eventually, I got tired of paying bills. I wanted to spend my money on myself, not on my creditors. I began to miss payments. Then I'd get charged a late fee, which could cost a lot—usually about $35 each time! Plus, because I had allowed the late charges and penalties to pile up, I was way over my credit limit. So I was also now paying an over-the-limit-fee of $25 each month.

I reached a point where I didn't care about paying my credit cards back. So I went from making late payments to making no payments at all. I hoped that somehow the bills would all just disappear, that they would pay themselves off.

But they never did. I got letter after letter telling me that if I didn't pay them back it would affect my credit rating, meaning that they would write up a report saying I was not good at paying back loans. I grew concerned. I wanted to get my own apartment in college. I knew that in order to have this, I had to have good credit. No landlord wants a tenant who doesn't pay his bills. There were also other things that I wanted, like a car and, one day, a house. The only way I was going to be able to repair my credit was to pay the bills that I'd ignored for so long.

> *It was amazing. With my credit cards whatever I wanted was mine. Five years later, I am still paying.*

By then, I owed the credit card companies $2,800. I began paying as much as I could every month, which was about $65 per card. But no matter how much I paid, it didn't make a dent in my debt.

Finally I heard about a debt management agency which would work with my creditors on negotiating lower interest rates for the amounts I owed. This would make it easier to keep up with my debt, and also help stop the annoying letters and phone calls that I was getting about my bills, as long as I paid the lower rates reliably. This would last for a couple of years, or until I paid off all the bills. (I was fortunate to find a trustworthy debt management agency, but beware: Many debt management operations are expensive, unreliable, or even fraudulent. See the end of this article for resources to help you avoid a scam.)

Five years later, I am still paying off the credit cards. Right now I owe about $1,300. I have cut up all my cards except for one, which I keep just in case I have an emergency.

It's a burden to have this debt, especially since I now live on my own. After I get done paying for rent, utilities, my phone, cable, food, transportation, credit cards, and other bills, I barely have $65 left to myself.

In addition, my credit is now messed up. Had I known that negative items stay on my credit report for seven years (yes, seven years!), I would have thought twice about not paying the bills back. Now, for the next seven years it will be very difficult for me to get a loan for a home or car.

Today, I am very cautious about how I spend my money. I try not to waste it on foolish items. I still want a house and a car, but if I don't clean up the mess I made when I was younger, it will never happen.

I truly resent credit cards now. I look at them as a trap, laced with everything your heart desires (or that your credit limit allows). And I don't even wear Adidas anymore.

*If you're in trouble with debt, the Federal Trade Commission offers advice on getting back on track at its website (go to ftc.gov/credit). In particular, see the FTC publications Choosing a Credit Counselor and Coping with Debt. They are available at the website or by calling toll-free: 1-877-FTC-HELP.*

---

*Xavier went on to college and graduate school, and got a job at a major media company.*

# How I Learned to Be Stingy

By Asia Fillmore

When your pockets are big, the amount of friends you have gets larger. But when your money gets low, your friend circle begins to shrink. I had to realize that only the ones who never leave your side are your true friends.

A couple of months ago I learned a lesson about my friends Mimi and Dem. Mimi was my girl; I knew her for a little while. And Dem was all her peoples that be over at her house all the time.

It was Friday—payday. Ever since I got my job at a department store, like clockwork Mimi was calling my phone Friday asking me when I'm gonna come on the block.

You know the saying, "If I eat then my friends eat"? Mimi and Dem thought it went, "If I eat, my friends eat. And then they mama and they grandmama can eat too!"

Mimi's house was the chill spot. She lived in a four-bedroom townhouse with her mama, her mama's boyfriend, her grandmama, her two little sisters and little brother, and one of her sister's babies. Mimi's older brother was locked up, but his baby mama lives there, too.

Mimi's house was crowded, but we always had fun sitting in the big living room or outside on the porch. Mimi and Dem were hoodrats, I knew that for a fact. But I still hung out with them, because when I moved to the area they were the first people I met and Mimi was popular around.

One Friday night Dem wanted to have a party at Mimi's house. They were telling me it was gonna be the bomb. Everybody had been askin' when Mimi gonna have another party at her house. They asked me did I wanna help put in on the party for food and liquor. They would be charging $10 to get in, so I would get my money back and then a little interest. I was like, "Cool, I definitely can use the money."

Me and Mimi went to the liquor store. Mimi was saying how they'd told mad people about the party on Facebook. Everybody, I mean everybody, was coming tonight.

We went in the liquor store and Mimi just started picking up bottles. She didn't have two pennies in her pocket to rub together. You would've thought she was balling, the way she was just dropping bottles in the cart, not even looking at prices. But I knew Mimi was broke as a joke.

*Ever since I got my job, like clockwork Mimi was calling on Friday—payday—asking me when I'm gonna come on the block.*

"Yo, you buggin, this mad money," I said.

She was like, "Damn, don't even trip; you gonna get ya money back ASAP."

We put all the bottles on the counter, and the total came up to $150. I shook my head and went into my wallet.

Mimi said, "Girl, I don't even know why you was trippin; you got mad money." Then she asked me to buy her a pack of cigarettes; she was gonna pay me back after the party.

I was spending money on this girl like we went together. I didn't mind because I was calculating in my head if 30 people came, that was $300; 50 people, $500. So that would be more than enough to get my money and a decent amount of interest.

We got back to the house and started moving stuff around. Since it was my money that paid for the liquor, I wanted to get mine before everybody. I opened the Ciroc and started throwing back shots.

In 15 minutes I was feeling it. I turned the music up blasting in the living room. Mimi wanted to be in charge of taking the money so she was supposed to be by the door. And Dem was scattered around doing their thing. I saw mad heads starting to come through the door. And I was still in the living room getting my $150 worth of fun.

The party was getting live early. Nobody was sitting down; everybody was dancing and having a good time. I was feeling good; I even had an idea that we could make this a business, be little entrepreneurs. Out on the dance floor, I saw Mimi backing it up on somebody. I moved over and asked her, "Mimi, ain't you suppose to be at the door?"

She got mad because the guy she was dancing with moved over and got behind another chick.

"Why you beastin?" she said. "My lil sister at the door."

I went to the front of the house. Mimi's sister wasn't at the door; nobody was. I opened it and her sister wasn't outside; neither was any of Dem. I stood in the doorway confused. Then this tall slinky guy tried to pass me and go in the house. I stopped him and said the party was $10.

"What you mean $10, I was just in here and I ain't have to pay $10."

I was furious. Somebody was going to run me my money: $150 needed to be paid in full plus interest. Not now but right now.

And then I saw the main culprit. In my mind, I pulled Mimi by her ponytail out the house and beat the living daylights out of her. Then I had to stop thinking with the right side of my head. If I was to start fighting Mimi in her house, everyone from her mama to her grandmother would be on me like white on rice. And then I definitely wouldn't be able to get my money back.

So I went in Mimi's room to my pocketbook that I'd hid under her bed. (I knew somebody in her family would go in my purse if they saw it lying around.) I checked to see if the rest of my money was there and then I went back and told her she needed to give me my money now 'cause I was going home.

She suddenly had all the excuses in the world. Saying, "Nobody knew the party wasn't free, so nobody brought no money. I didn't want the party to be booty so I just let them all in for free."

I was flabbergasted. "Well, somebody in this house need to run me my money. The agreement was for me to pay for the alcohol, and I get my money back plus interest."

"Asia, I swear we gonna get you your money back; don't trip."

"How, Mimi? You ain't got no job."

She then said she swore on her great-grandmother's grave. I wasn't hearing that. Ain't nothing else could happen to her great-grandmother. I needed her to say this on somebody that's living.

"Asia, you know I got you. I wouldn't even play you like that." She tapped my shoulders and then walked away.

I walked out the house ashamed and embarrassed. I felt played. I guess I was one of Dem, except I was out $150. I'd wasted almost half my paycheck. And I still needed to wash clothes, pay my cell phone bill ($120), and go food shopping. I now had to stretch my money for a week.

I didn't have family around to spot me $20 whenever I needed it. It was me alone, and I work hard for my money. Standing on my feet eight hours a day, five days a week. I caught a cab, went home, and fell asleep real uneasy.

The next day I called Mimi and asked her when I was going to get my money 'cause I really needed it. Mimi told me that she would have my money that Friday, a week later. After work that night I went straight to her house. Her mother answered the door and said Mimi had just left. She didn't know when she would be home.

The next day I saw Mimi and Dem walking up the street.

Dem didn't look especially fly, but Mimi was wearing new Jordans, an Ed Hardy hat, a new shirt, and a fresh pair of jeans.

I didn't confront her when I saw her; I didn't want to. I just wanted her to be a civilized person and give me my money. How hard was that? She knew she was wrong.

*Now I know that if people were really my friends they wouldn't get mad at me if I didn't buy them something.*

I had other friends but they weren't as popular as Mimi. I didn't want to hang around them because I felt they weren't as cool. But when me and Mimi and Dem went our separate ways after that party, I realized that other people I knew were way better than Mimi. They didn't mooch off of me and they were actually nicer to be around.

I used to throw money away, do everything to please someone else. Now I know that if people were really my friends they wouldn't get mad at me if I didn't buy them something from the store. They wouldn't want to call me just when I had money. We would be together all week long, not just Friday to Sunday.

Mimi never did pay me back.

---

*Asia was 19 when she wrote this story. She got her GED and went to William Paterson College.*

# The Basics of Account-Ability

By Darnise Gilbert

I interviewed Clare Stenstrom, a certified financial planner in New York City, to find out how youth starting out on their own can become financially stable. Here's her advice:

**Step One: Open a Bank Account**

Shop around to find a bank that offers a low- or no-fee checking account. Having a bank account will help you establish good credit, which will help you when you need to rent an apartment or want a credit card or a car loan. Just be sure you don't write a check for money you don't have, or get caught paying a lot of fees for ATM or other withdrawals.

**Step Two: Make a Budget**

For two months, write down every cent you actually spend, and compare what you're earning and spending. Do you have money left over after your expenditures? Whether or not you do, it's best to put money away before you start spending. Set a goal (e.g., first and last month's rent plus security deposit) and then figure out how much of each paycheck you'll have to save to meet that goal.

The key to budgeting is prioritizing your most important expenses. So, look at your list of costs over the two months and write down all your most important items: rent, utilities, and a minimum phone bill, as well as transportation, food, work clothes, cleaning and personal care products. These are your priorities. Below this list, make a "things that make life better" list—cable TV, vacations, entertainment, etc. Below that, put your "treats" list—things like fancy handheld devices or dinners out.

*If you're not earning enough to cover your expenses with 70% of your paycheck, it's time to make cutbacks.*

If you're not earning enough money to cover all your expenses with 70% of your paycheck, it's time to make some cutbacks. Begin with the things on the bottom of your list (the "treats"). Some day when you really need money, you'll be glad you made these sacrifices and saved instead.

## Step Three: Don't Buy Without Thinking

If you see something you really like that is not within your budget, wait 24 hours to see if you still want it. If you do, research the item on the Internet and call other stores to see if you can find it cheaper somewhere else.

Make a list of pros and cons about every big purchase you're considering. For example, the cons of buying a TV might be that it costs a lot and you won't be able to afford other things from your "things that make life better" list. But a pro might be that it will save you money because you'll watch it instead of spending money going out.

## Step Four: Find Small Ways to Save

Small wastes of money really add up. A cold bottle of water might cost you $1.50 in a deli, but you can buy it by the case for 25 cents a bottle and refrigerate it yourself. Figure out how much you spend on coffee and food: Preparing food at home is not only healthier, it's cheaper. If you have a cell phone, get the cheapest plan that works for you, and stay within it. You can save hundreds of dollars a year just making little changes like these.

### Step Five: Watch Your Transportation Expenses

Cars are very expensive to buy and operate. Insurance, gas, oil changes, tune-ups, and replacement parts can easily run $200 a month—and that's not counting your car payment (if you have a loan). That's why it's a good idea to use public transportation if at all possible. If not, call your insurance company to find out if you can lower the cost of your car insurance by taking a driver's education course. An online class can often save you 10% or more.

If you absolutely must have a car for work, it makes more sense to buy a really good used car than a new one. New cars lose up to 20% of their value the minute you drive them off the showroom floor.

### Step Six: Avoid Lending Money

Friendships and families can be destroyed if one person doesn't pay another back or doesn't pay them back on time. If you do lend money, make sure the person has a way to pay you back. Also, you should both sign a note that says when they borrowed the money and when they will return it. Remember that it costs money to lend money. Your money could be earning interest for you in the bank while the other person has it.

---

*Darnise was 20 when she wrote this story.*

# Secondhand, First-Rate

### By Anita Ames

It wasn't just a regular "I Love New York" T-shirt. The letters were made out of all different colors of velvet and the words went straight across the shirt instead of one under the other. It was super exclusive. I had to ask my co-worker, Ernest, where he'd gotten it.

"Beacon's Closet. A thrift store in Williamsburg, Brooklyn," he said.

I could never see myself shopping at a thrift store, so I didn't think much more about it. But the next day when I walked into my job at the Brooklyn Children's Museum, Ernest had on yet another great item—a blue jacket with a yellow hood and blue drawstrings, large pockets and a metal zipper. Once again, he said he'd bought it at Beacon's Closet. He also told me you could trade and sell your clothes there. Now I wanted to know more. "What are the store hours? When can I go?" I asked.

That weekend I went to the store and tried to sell all of my old clothes. But the store clerks discarded all of my items. They said my jeans were too worn-out, that cords didn't sell well at the store, and that my shirts weren't vintage enough. I was really upset because my impression of thrift stores was that they only sold worn-out clothes that no one wanted anymore. Why wouldn't they take mine? But the clerks said I could leave my clothes there to be donated to charity, so I did.

I decided to look around the store for clothes anyway. I went to the denim section and saw a whole bunch of expensive name-brand jeans. When I looked at the price tags, I couldn't believe my eyes. A pair I liked were only $21! The jeans looked fairly new and some even still had tags on them. Now it made sense that they hadn't bought my worn-out jeans.

*I thought it would be stupid to give up the chance to buy jeans for less than half price.*

My friends were kind of skeptical about the store. "How do you know those jeans are real? They could be bootleg for all you know," they said. Some even said, "Ew, someone else's clothes? That's so nasty."

But I knew the jeans were real because they had the same tags that were in my jeans that I'd bought for $100 at an expensive department store. The idea of wearing other people's clothes did bother me at first, but I knew I could easily wash the clothes at home. I thought it would be stupid to give up the chance to buy jeans for less than half the price they would be in regular stores.

The next time I went to Beacon's Closet to sell clothes, I took some of my best attire that I didn't wear anymore. I brought in an Adidas track jacket that I'd paid $85 for, and a pair of Coach loafers that had cost me $130. The store bought both the jacket and shoes.

At first I felt cheated because I only got about $15 in cash. But then I bought a Michael Kors T-shirt for $8 (it must have cost more than $70 new) and some fierce vintage sunglasses for $3. So in the end I think it evened out, and I ended up with some great new (well, old) items.

---

*Anita was 18 when she wrote this story. She went on to attend SUNY Albany.*

# Swap and Save

By Anita Ames

Affordable, good-quality clothes are hard to come by, especially if you're a teen who makes little or no money. But there is a way to get those clothes you've been looking for—for free. And the best part is that they may be right in your mom's, friend's, or co-worker's closet already.

When I told the editors at my teen journalism program about my excitement about thrift stores, one of them began to tell me about clothing swaps. She said that once a year, she and her friends come together with clothes they don't want anymore and swap them. It sounded like a great opportunity to get good clothes for free.

I decided to hold a clothing swap of my own at the journalism program's office. I put up some flyers around the office inviting writers and other staff to the swap, and telling them to bring any clothes they didn't want anymore.

When the day of the swap arrived, I brought in a pair of jeans that had been my favorite in 5th grade (they didn't quite fit anymore), a pair of Coach shoes I hadn't been able to sell to a thrift store, and some shirts with logos on them that I no longer wore. I couldn't wait to get some new clothes.

First, my editor and I made labels for the different categories of clothing, like shirts, jeans, sweaters, etc. We put them on different areas of a big table so that it was easier for people to look through specific types of clothing instead of having everything in one large, messy pile.

People brought in such a variety of items that I wasn't worried about anyone fighting over clothes. Even if someone didn't get the shirt they really wanted, a pair of cool shorts lurked nearby. I just wanted everyone to leave with at least one item they liked, and to have fun.

We did. About seven people showed up and we all tried on a bunch of outfits. Everyone got at least one item and had fun in the process. My fellow teen writer Viveca picked out a cute pink top and a red and black scarf. "You win some and lose some," she said, "and I won some today."

Another writer, Shameeka, got a pair of green pants that she looked absolutely stunning in. My editor swapped her blazer and skirt for Viveca's spaceship T-shirt. Suddenly she had a great new sporty look.

A s for myself, I tried on my editor's royal blue blazer and I liked how it fit me. I ended up leaving with more items than I'd come with. I got the blazer, plus a couple of skirts, a pair of off-white pants, a pink halter top, some Adidas sweats to wear around my dorm at college, and a green blouse. I was more than satisfied.

When I asked some of the other participants why they had come, one of them said, "Clothing swaps are great because they let you experiment with styles of clothing you'd never think to wear and, before you know it, you have a new look." She was right. I never would have worn a pink halter top with gold beads before, but when I tried it on at the swap I ended up really liking it. It fit great and I knew I could find cute sandals to go with it for summer.

If you're thinking of hosting a clothing swap, there are some things you should keep in mind. One is to make sure the clothes that are being swapped are clean and undamaged. Also, make sure to specify what you want people to bring to the swap, like jeans, shorts, shirts, accessories, and shoes, but no undergarments or worn bathing suits. My editor also suggested that you should "make sure there's a variety of clothes to suit all different shapes and sizes."

I agree. If there are some larger people at the swap, it won't be fair if everything there is too small for them. My advice is to invite people of all different body types so that everyone can leave the swap happy. And if two people want the same item, a fair way to decide who gets it is a simple game of rock, paper, scissors.

*Invite people of all different body types so that everyone can leave the swap happy.*

Also keep in mind that the clothing swap will most likely be with people that you work with, go to school with, or otherwise see often. "You have to make sure that if you swap with friends or colleagues, you feel comfortable wearing their clothes to work or school," said Marie, another editor. I definitely agree, because there's nothing worse than feeling out of place with a co-worker's jeans on. But I also think that clothes are all about your personality; you can transform the clothes you wear as much as they transform you. I'm just afraid that I'll look so good in a friend's shirt, she might want it back.

---

*Anita was 18 when she wrote this story. She went on to attend SUNY Albany..*

# How Am I Supposed to Pay for College?

### By Maria Alashola

They tell you that going to college should be the only thing on your mind. They tell you that not going to college is the worst thing in the world. But as I head into 11th grade, I have no idea about how to choose, get into, and especially, how to pay for college. My family is financially unstable, and I don't live with my parents. I don't know how you find out about scholarships, or even how to choose a college.

I did a bit of online research in the beginning of the summer and got interested in Stanford, a private college in California. But when I told my friend about Stanford, she nearly laughed in my face. With more research I realized why.

Stanford wasn't a realistic idea, it was a dream school. One year of tuition, room and board, and other expenses at Stanford costs $60,749, according to Stanford.edu. Where was I going to get a quarter million dollars to pay for all four years? It's very competitive, too: How did people even get into this school? How did people get into any college at all? Then I found the help I needed online.

Colleges generally are just for undergraduates. Universities offer graduate degrees like master's degrees and doctorates. Sometimes they have several colleges within them.

The College Board's Big Future website explains it well at **bigfuture.collegeboard.org/find-colleges/college-101/types-of-colleges-the-basics**. In fact, it's worth spending some time on that website, **bigfuture.collegeboard.org**, because it provides an easy-to-navigate overview of planning for college.

From that site I learned that public colleges get state and federal government money and have lower tuition, especially for in-state students. Private colleges raise their money from tuition and donations. Public college seems like the better deal if you don't have much money, but if you love a particular private school, check out what kind of scholarship money you could get.

For-profit schools, also known as proprietary schools, are operated by private, profit-seeking businesses. Their recruitment tactics can be aggressive, so be careful when you are recruited by these types of schools. They tend to cost a lot more than comparable public colleges, and students are likelier to end up defaulting on their loans.

To find out if a school is for-profit, go to: **nces.ed.gov/collegenavigator**. Type in your school's name, and you can see, in the third line, if it says "for-profit." You can also click on the bottom category, "Cohort Default Rates" and see how many students were unable to pay back their loans. A higher number means a lot of students either didn't graduate or couldn't get a good enough job to pay back the loans they needed for tuition. Also, keep in mind that college credits from these schools are often impossible to transfer to a four-year school. (The NCES site also provides lots of other information about admission requirements, costs, courses, and more for any school in the country.)

*For-profit schools tend to cost a lot more than comparable public colleges, and students are likelier to end up defaulting on their loans.*

Community colleges are two-year schools that often get a bad rap, but they can be a great place to start. If you get good grades there, you can transfer to a four-year college. Other types of two-year schools are vocational colleges, which prepare you for specific professions in fields like technology or culinary arts or medical assistant. Often they offer job placement at the end of the two years. Many two-year public colleges offer these programs at a much lower price than the trade schools that advertise on buses and subways.

F ederal Student Aid is part of the Department of Education, which distributes $150 billion to college students every year. **FAFSA** is the Free Application for Federal Student Aid. To receive financial aid, you must start with this form. The application becomes available on January 1, and the sooner you fill it out the better. So, instead of going to count down the ball on New Year's Eve, you should count down the seconds before the application opens. Go to **fafsa.ed.gov** to get started.

Once your information is in the FAFSA system, you become eligible to apply for several types of grants, loans, and even on-campus work study jobs that can help you pay your way through college.

A grant is money that you don't have to pay back, but you may have to maintain a certain grade point average to keep getting it. A loan, on the other hand, you have to pay back whether or not you complete your education—plus interest. (Interest is a fee you pay for borrowing money.) A work study job is a part-time position that you can receive while you are enrolled in college. Work study jobs help you earn money to cover your additional college expenses such as books, traveling, and supplies. Work study jobs can be anywhere on campus from the bookstore to the cafeteria to the administration office. There are a limited number of these slots, so make sure to contact your college's work study office as soon as you are admitted.

In terms of different types of grants, there's the **Pell Grant**, a federal grant offered to college students. You need to have completed your FAFSA to get it. The amount of money you will receive depends on your financial need and if you are attending college full-time or part-time. Like all grants, the Pell Grant doesn't have to be repaid—no interest or anything! According to studentaid.ed.gov the maximum amount a student can receive per year is $5,550. Every school offers this money.

For youth in foster care, perhaps the most important resource after the Pell is the **ETV**, which stands for Education Training Voucher. It is a national, federally funded program that helps youth in foster care with college costs. The maximum you can receive is $5,000 per year for school expenses, including tuition, books, housing, and transportation. In New York, you must apply before you're 21, and you can keep getting ETV up until your 23rd birthday. You have to fill out a separate application to get an ETV. Ask your caseworker where to get it (applications become available in July).

Another grant that you might receive (more money that does not need to be paid back) after completing FAFSA is **FSEOG** which stands for Federal Supplemental Educational Opportunity Grant. It is for students with exceptional financial need. You can get between $100 and $4,000 a year. Yana Geyfman, a college counselor from Goddard Riverside's Options Center in New York, who I met with, mentioned that the government's supply of FSEOG money runs out quickly. The

*Federal loans are better to take out than regular bank loans because the interest is lower, and subsidized federal loans are better than unsubsidized loans.*

earlier you apply for this, the more likely you are to get some of this money. Not every college offers FSEOG, so ask the financial aid office at the college you are interested in. Find information on your states' financial aid office at **www2.ed.gov/sgt**.

To get a state grant, you must be a resident of the state. You can apply for state aid directly from your FAFSA confirmation page, though you may have to add more information in a separate application.

Scholarships are similar to grants in that you don't have to pay back the money, but they may require more than just showing need. Scholarships go to students who play a sport, get good grades, or have a special skill. There are even a few scholarships just for youth in foster care. Start your research early so you can have time to apply for many different types of scholarships. Get help from a knowledgeable staff member or counselor if you can.

There are several good websites such as **bigfuture. collegeboard.org/scholarship-search** and **fastweb.com**. Most colleges also have their own scholarships—some require a separate application and some don't. Check your school's website.

You can get federal loans from the government or private loans from banks or other companies. Yana explained that federal loans are better to take out than regular bank loans because the interest is lower. She further explained that federal loans come in two categories, subsidized and unsubsidized loans. The government pays interest on subsidized loans while you attend college, but does not do so for unsubsidized loans. You have a choice of paying off an unsubsidized loan yourself while you attend college or waiting to pay it off after you graduate.

How much loan money you can get depends on your answers to FAFSA questions. Learn more at **studentaid.ed.gov/types/ loans/subsidized-unsubsidized**. But remember—just because you are eligible does not mean you should take out a loan. You have to pay it back.

After my research and talking to Yana, I felt less stressed about the whole college process. I realized maybe college isn't just for rich kids. There are ways to pay for an education; you just need to know where to look.

---

*Maria was 16 when she wrote this story.*

# Scam U.: For-Profit Colleges May Rip You Off

By Marco Salazar

Early in my senior year of high school, I went to English class and found that a representative of DeVry University would lead the day's "lesson." The representative said he would be giving us tips on the college search process.

He handed out electronic devices to everyone in the room and had us use them to play a game. We were all supposed to be running a business and had to make decisions about where to spend money. Everyone participated excitedly and competitively.

Afterwards, he collected the devices and said, "At DeVry we like to use technology like this to enhance learning." Then he went around the room asking questions like, "Who would you make proud by attending college?" and, "What can college offer you?" He then asked us whether our parents had gone to college and if not, what jobs they had.

He was indirectly suggesting that our parents who hadn't gone to college weren't successful, and that we, too, would end up that way if we didn't go to college. This representative did not give us a single helpful tip for the college search process; instead he advertised DeVry all period and attempted to convince my class that college, specifically DeVry, should be our next step.

Why was he being allowed to preempt my English class to give me a sales pitch? To my knowledge, only one other college had visited my school—CUNY's Macaulay Honors College—and they held an optional information session after school. They didn't interrupt our class time. (According to a New York City Department of Education spokesperson, the department does not allow these visits during the school day.) Nor did Macaulay show off devices in a shallow attempt to appeal to youth, particularly low-income youth.

I'd seen DeVry advertised on TV and the subway, and my friends had made fun of it a few times, so I knew it wasn't exactly a top school. Watching their representative talk to my class, I was able to identify certain advertising techniques I'd learned about in school. For example, we'd been taught that advertisers use fear to manipulate people's decisions. The representative was clearly trying to scare students about the consequences of not attending college—to scare them into considering DeVry.

The only thing I didn't understand was why DeVry was working so hard to recruit students, while the schools I was interested in attending more or less let applicants come to them. So I did some research at home. I figured that DeVry was a low-tier school trying to round up students who didn't have a lot of other options. I suspected they recruited at high schools like mine, where many students are low-income minorities who have trouble getting into and affording college.

*Students at for-profit schools take out more federal student aid and are much less likely to repay their loans.*

It turns out my suspicions were correct. But the case against DeVry—and a lot of similar colleges—was much stronger than I'd thought.

It turns out that DeVry is a for-profit college. What does that mean? You might not think much of this fact at first—after all, traditional colleges are often so expensive that their "nonprofit" status is hard to understand.

The difference is that for-profit colleges have owners—either private families, or companies, or stock market shareholders—whose main intention is to make money. A for-profit college's first responsibility is to its owners or shareholders, so it may focus more on making a profit than on your quality of education. A nonprofit college, on the other hand, has no owner and has more incentive to focus on graduating satisfied students. In fact, many schools receive big donations from alumni who feel their college education contributed to their success in life.

Complaints from students at for-profit colleges suggest what can go wrong when student success is not a college's first priority. Students who filed a lawsuit against the for-profit Everest College told the current affairs TV program Frontline that they graduated from a $30,000 nursing program without ever setting foot inside a hospital. The students claimed their education was a huge rip-off, because they were effectively unhireable as graduates.

Another lawsuit involving student loan fraud resulted in DeVry paying out $88,122 to students. After an investigation by the New York State Attorney General, DeVry admitted that it had steered students into taking out loans from Citibank, and in return the school received a commission from the bank for each loan made. This violated the Attorney General's College Code of Conduct, because the practice meant that students weren't informed of other loan sources that might have given them better deals.

Meanwhile, the outlook for graduates of for-profit colleges is often bleak. The U.S. Department of Education has released figures showing that, compared to students at other colleges, students at for-profit schools take out more federal student aid and are much less likely to repay their loans. This may mean that the for-profit colleges' students aren't getting good jobs after graduating, or that these colleges prey on students who are in bad financial circumstances in the first place (most likely, it means both).

Some for-profit schools are blunt about targeting vulnerable people. When a Senate oversight committee investigated the for-profit industry, it obtained a document in which leaders at Vatterott Educational Centers, Inc., told employees, "We serve the UN-DER world" — that is, the "Unemployed, Underpaid, Unsatisfied, Unskilled, Unprepared, Unsupported, Unmotivated, Unhappy, Underserved!"

The committee also found that training documents from another for-profit, the ITT Technical Institute, included a "Pain Funnel and Pain Puzzle" — a set of instructions advising recruiters on how to stimulate negative emotional responses, such as regret, to manipulate students to enroll.

*Getting into a for-profit school is as easy as getting a store to take your money.*

Following the investigations of the Senate oversight committee, Congress passed a bill in 2011 placing stricter regulations on for-profit colleges. (Some of its provisions were overturned by a federal judge in 2012.) One of the new policies forces career colleges to tell students upfront about the school's graduation rate, success at placing graduates in jobs, and students' median debt load. This information can help prospective students make informed decisions, and avoid colleges that seem to have lots of dropouts who leave with tons of debt.

K nowing all this, I don't see why anyone would want to pay high tuition to a for-profit college when they could attend community college instead. Community colleges offer many of the programs for-profit schools offer at a fraction of the price.

I'm not sure if students realize this, or realize that for-profit colleges generally have the same open-admissions policy as most two-year community colleges: They accept just about everyone who applies.

In fact, I did a quick search on Facebook (using the "search posts by everyone" feature), looking for the phrase "accepted to DeVry." I figured that people who were excited about attending this college would be likely to mention it in a status update. Sure enough, my search turned up many people—most of them minorities—happily announcing their acceptance.

In reality, getting into a for-profit school is as easy as getting a store to take your money. My advice is to avoid attending a for-profit school. Not all are guilty of the practices described above, but they all require you to pay for something you could get for less money elsewhere. Employers are unlikely to see any difference between a degree from DeVry and a degree from a community college. In fact, they might even question your judgment for choosing a for-profit school over a much cheaper community college.

Not once during the DeVry presentation at my school did the representative even mention that it's a for-profit institution. Perhaps he didn't want us to uncover the investigations surrounding the school. Nor did anyone at my school ever warn my classmates or me against taking out big loans to attend for-profit schools. So I'm warning you now: Don't become prey.

---

*Marco graduated high school and went to Massachusetts Institute of Technology (MIT).*

## Start Your Search Here

As you consider your college options, go to nces.ed.gov/collegenavigator. Provided by the U.S. Department of Education, this online tool lets you quickly view lots of important information about any college in the country.

To judge whether a college represents value for your money, take a look at the "Cohort Default Rates" category. This shows you the percentage of recent graduates who have been unable to pay back their student loans in a given year. At some colleges, this rate is close to 0%—indicating that former students earn enough to cover living expenses and student loans comfortably.

At others, the default rate may be 10%, 20%, or even higher. Be extremely wary of colleges with such high default rates, which suggest that a college is not giving its students the education they need to make a living while repaying loans. (According to a 2010 story in The Chronicle of Higher Education, 40% of loans taken out by students at for-profit colleges are in default—that is, the students are unable to repay them—after 15 years. For a list of the 20 for-profit colleges with the highest default rates, go to chronicle.com/article/For-Profit-Colleges-Face-Risk/66215.)

The college navigator tool also lets you look at statistics like graduation rates, percentage of students returning after freshman year, net price, and percentages of students receiving different types of financial aid. These figures will give you a good idea of how much academic and financial support you're likely to receive at a particular college. If the graduation rate is low, it's a sign that many students struggle.

Meanwhile, you'll be better off at a college where students get more of their financial aid in the form of grants and scholarships (which don't have to be repaid) and less in the form of student loans (which do need to be repaid and can be a long-term financial burden).

A lot of the figures you find won't mean much on their own—to understand whether a college is doing well or badly in a certain category, you'll need to look at lots of colleges (preferably different kinds) and compare them. So get online and start navigating!

# Take Charge of Your College Bills

By Marci Bayer

Many college students struggle not only to pay tuition, but also to figure out financial aid forms, choose loans, and limit spending once they get to college. To find out more about navigating these challenges, I interviewed Jane Heaphy, the director of Goddard Riverside's Options Center, who has more than 17 years of experience counseling students, to get her advice on managing finances in college.

**Q: What should students do when they get to college to make sure they're on top of their financial aid?**

**A:** Meet with your financial aid counselor in person just to say, "Can we go over my plan so I'm really clear on it?" You want to feel educated on the aid you're receiving, because you're going to have to renew your financial aid every single year. Also, if the financial aid staff knows you and they can go the extra mile for you, that's a good investment of your time.

**Q: What's the most common source of confusion when it comes to financial aid?**

**A:** You're filling out forms that go to the state government and federal government. The government agencies give you many months to complete the forms, but the colleges themselves require that you complete the forms by a "priority deadline." The priority deadline for each college varies, but is usually in February or March. Unless you file your FAFSA (application for federal aid) by the priority deadline, colleges may not consider you for maximum aid. So it's really important students know the priority financial aid deadline at each of their colleges. You

> *Send a letter saying, 'I'd like you to consider me for additional financial aid,' and explain more about your life situation.*

can find it on the college website or call the college financial aid office.

Another important thing to know is that "financial aid" includes grants (which are scholarships and do not need to be paid back), loans (which need to be paid back with interest), and work study (a campus job that pays you a wage like any other job). When a school tells you, "We'll cover your full financial aid," you still want to know: What kind of aid is it, how much are you borrowing, how much can you expect to earn in a job once you're there?

**Q: Can you offer any advice for dealing with the bureaucracy of financial aid offices?**

A: Keep a paper trail—a copy of your FAFSA and letters from the college, so you have a fat folder of all your financial aid information. If there's some problem, you want to be able to defend your situation by having all your documents.

**Q: What can students do if financial aid doesn't meet all their expenses?**

A: Apply to a range of schools, so hopefully you'll have one school that's affordable. You can also advocate for yourself. Send a letter saying, "I'd like you to consider me for additional financial aid," and explain more about your life situation. Sometimes it works and sometimes it doesn't, but it's an effort of 15 minutes writing the letter, and if you get $2,000 more, it was worth it.

Also, sometimes in July and August there are kids they thought were going to come to school who aren't. Those students were allocated a certain amount of financial aid and now it's going back in the pot, and the college is going to give it out again. You want to make sure you're on a list to get that additional aid, so talk to the financial aid office about it.

### Q: Would you advise students to take out loans?

**A:** It depends. If my choice was to take out some loans or not go to college, I would advise everybody to take out some loans. However, I want students to feel really informed about what their responsibilities are. If after you leave college you're spending, say, $1,200 a month paying back your loans, then it may have been counterproductive. There are some loan calculators on finaid.org that will help you break the total amount you're considering into the monthly amounts you'll pay for 10 years. I find those helpful.

### Q: How should a student evaluate different types of loans?

**A:** Loans from the federal loan program have the lowest interest rates and make the most sense. Then there are private loans, from different financial institutions. In my experience, if you're getting into the private loan area, you probably want to reconsider. With the federal loan program, you can get up to about $24,000 per year. If you're borrowing more than that, I would be very cautious.

### Q: What should students do to manage their money in college?

**A:** When you get to college, credit cards are almost thrown at you, when you actually don't have the ability to pay up yet. It can become an all-consuming kind of debt. So be educated about credit cards, and learn money-saving tips from students who've been there a couple of years already. Buy books online or from other students. If you've already paid for your meal plan, eat in the cafeteria. Additionally, you have to pay for the occasional tube of toothpaste or the bus ticket home, so make sure that you open a bank account when you get to campus.

**Q: What do you advise for those who must work to pay for school?**

A: Certainly the extra cash can keep the pressure off. I also think it can get you more connected on campus if you get a work study job—those can be good networking opportunities. It becomes a problem when you're working so much that you can't be the student you want to be. Plan it out so that your hours are as part-time as possible.

**Q: What's most important to remember when dealing with finances during college?**

A: Before you sign a loan or fill out forms, don't be afraid to ask questions. So much of the time, we think we're supposed to know things, but actually it's new to us. New college students are all learning about financial aid, so it's critical to ask questions.

---

*Marci was 16 when she wrote this story. She went on
to attend the University of Maryland.*

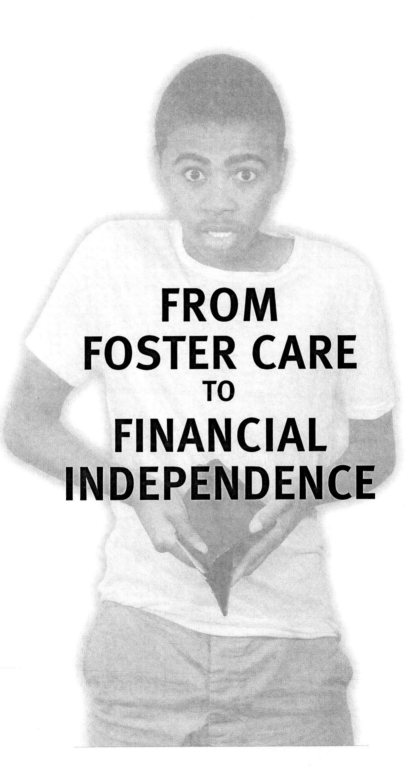

# FROM
# FOSTER CARE
## TO
# FINANCIAL
# INDEPENDENCE

# On My Own: An Aging Out Story

By Anonymous

Although it's illegal in New York state for a foster child to age out into homelessness, sometimes there's nowhere else to go. Sometimes going to a shelter or living on the streets are the only choices. As I approached my 21st birthday, this was very much on my mind.

The year before I aged out, I went to a workshop that was supposed to prepare me. One of the guest speakers was a young man named Peter who'd been in kinship care with his aunt. He told us that his aunt had promised she wouldn't put him out on the street, but on his 21st birthday, that's just what she did. He started sleeping on the trains.

Over dinner that night, my foster mother Patricia and I talked about my meeting. I started crying because I was scared that I was going to end up in a shelter. Patricia said that she was going to make a room in the basement for me and not to worry. "I wouldn't let you be in the street," she reassured me.

I'd been living in Patricia's home for three years. She had been caring and supportive and said she wanted the best for me. But I wasn't sure if I could trust her. She didn't always give me my allowance when she said she would. I'd also seen her intimidate some of the other girls by threatening to kick them out, then saying that she would let them stay. Sometimes she'd start an argument with me, trying to provoke me to disrespect her. She'd always apologize the next day, but it made me doubt her sometimes. What if she betrayed my trust like Peter's aunt did?

I started looking for a job and working with my caseworkers and lawyers. Over the spring and summer, I applied to more than 60 jobs but I didn't receive one phone call back. Patricia kept pressuring me to get a job.

My birthday is in December, so by fall, I was under a lot of pressure. Then I got a job at the Gap making more than minimum wage. I was proud of myself. But a month before I aged out, my hours started getting cut.

*I applied to more than 60 jobs but I didn't receive one phone call back.*

Patricia pressured me to get a second job as a home health aide, which was one of her jobs. But I didn't want to do that. I had spent a lot of hours in the Veteran's Hospital taking care of my uncle before he died. That job seemed too depressing; it would bring up a lot of sad memories. She complained about my Gap job not being a "real job" because I wasn't getting enough hours. My trust in her began to turn to animosity.

I had already applied for public housing; in New York, people aging out of care get a slight advantage in getting those apartments. But the waiting lists are still long. I knew that I might need a place to stay until things fell into place.

So before my discharge conference—the meeting with my caseworker to decide where I'd live after aging out—Patricia and I made a deal that I could continue to live with her after I aged out of care, and pay her rent. I knew it was important to put things in writing, so I wrote her a letter saying I would pay her $250 every month.

She said that was too low; she wanted $400. I told her $250 was all I could afford.

She shrugged her shoulders and raised her eyebrows and her voice. "I don't care if you don't like it. You can go to your uncle's house or the shelter." She lifted up her hand to signal she didn't want to talk about it anymore. I was so upset that I didn't eat my dinner.

The next day, I called my cousins and my uncle to ask if I could stay with them, but they all said that they didn't have space. (I had only met my father once and didn't know where he was; living with my mother was not an option.) They were sympathetic and wished me the best of luck.

It hurt to hear family say I couldn't stay with them. They told me to try to talk with Patricia. My uncle pointed out that Patricia wanted money. "Suggest she lower the $400 rate to $300. Work with her." I followed their advice and negotiated $300 rent, which was still a lot for me.

My discharge conference happened a few weeks before my birthday. My caseworker was worried that my foster mother might change her mind and not let me stay with her after all. At the conference, though, Patricia was sweet and said that she would let me stay. She didn't say anything about my paying rent.

I thought seriously about going to a shelter, even though that terrified me and I would lose so much comfort. In Patricia's house, I ate good food, watched cable TV, and relaxed in comfortable surroundings. In the shelter, I'd be living with strangers without any privacy.

I aged out on December 28th. Two days later Patricia asked for the rent, and I gave it to her. The payment plan was me paying her $150 every two weeks. But with my hours cut at the Gap, I couldn't pay the full amount of the second payment.

*Be consistent and persistent. Get a job, no matter how low-paying or odd.*

Patricia pushed me to apply for food stamps and threatened to kick me out if I didn't get them. Then she started accusing me of stealing her money. She'd say that I hadn't turned off the computer and was leaving the lights on all night. I wasn't doing those things.

Normally when I got stressed out, I'd buy a bus ticket to New Jersey and visit friends and relatives, but I couldn't afford to. Patricia had acted before like she cared about me, but now she only seemed to care about her money. I felt as if I needed to be completely independent and not rely on anyone else. I felt like nobody cared about me.

In late January, I saw my public housing apartment for the first time and absolutely loved it. But it would be more than a month before I could move in. During that time, Patricia's behavior changed for the worse. Around the middle of February, we got into a fight. She grabbed me and scratched me, and threatened to call the cops to put me out. Her sons got between us and told her to leave me alone. For the next few weeks, I kept my distance and paid my rent on time.

In March, my apartment was finally ready. I packed all my things and left my foster mother's house in a cab. I had no furniture but the agency provided a furniture voucher for $1,800, which I used for my first month's rent and security deposit. My rent when I moved in was $83, based on my pay stubs from the Gap.

My foster care caseworker helped me sign up for food stamps and health insurance (Medicaid) once I aged out. Food stamps cover food but not things like toilet paper, dishes, detergent, and toiletries.

In May I got a job at Wendy's, and I was still getting a few hours at the Gap, so I had two jobs to fall back on and started saving money every week. I also started selling products for Avon. That made me feel like a businesswoman.

But then I was fired from the Gap, and I quit Wendy's because they were also cutting my hours. Then I owed Avon $200 because a customer didn't pay for her merchandise—you have to buy from Avon what you sell. I had to tap into my savings since it wasn't enough to pay off the Avon bill.

I decided the best way to be financially secure was to go back to school so I could get a better-paying job. I enrolled in a two-year college and got a work study job at the Student Union, which helped me save money. Now I have 10 credits left until I graduate with my associate's degree. I'd like to transfer and get a bachelor's in teaching, so I could be a kindergarten teacher.

In the last year or so I've been earning a little here, a little there. I cleaned an office occasionally, and now I am an assistant to a lawyer seven or eight hours a week; I file documents and type affidavits and tax forms for $10 an hour. I found that job on Craigslist. I also go door-to-door to campaign for a city council-man for $8 an hour for 16-20 hours a week.

Being so close to getting my associate's makes me feel more hopeful about my future. What I went through aging out has shown me that I can handle a lot, and it also taught me to be more diplomatic.

My advice to young people about to age out: Bug your case-workers about your housing application; be consistent and per-sistent. Get a job, no matter how low-paying or odd, because the housing people will need to see pay stubs. And if possible, try to negotiate a good relationship with your foster parent because you may need her when you age out.

---

*The author is still in her apartment and working several jobs while she works toward her degree.*

# Countdown to Independence

By Giselle John

My next birthday is D-Day: I turn 21 and age out of the foster care system. That means I'll be living on my own and will have to be able to support myself.

I know this has been coming for a long time, and I've been looking forward to it with longing and anxiety. I have planned everything about aging out, from budgeting my money to apartment hunting. This is not to say that I'm totally ready to be living on my own. In fact, I'm nervous about it. But I'm also confident that things will work out because I know I've planned well.

I began to lay the groundwork for the day I age out of the system when I was 19. I got my first job, at Dress Barn, and opened a bank account so I could begin to save money.

Even though my job didn't pay much (it was minimum wage) and constantly tested my patience, I considered it better than nothing. Many times I wanted to quit (sometimes I still do), but that's not how the real world runs. I knew I needed to save money for my future: I'd been budgeting how much I would spend each month on rent, food, phone, entertainment, transportation, and clothes when I was on my own. I'd figured out it was going to be costly.

When I turned 20, I had one full year of planning left before I aged out. That's when I really started some serious evaluations. I asked myself questions like: Where do I want to live? How much rent do I want to pay? How much money do I need to save? Do I want to share an apartment with a roommate?

I also started paying attention to how people who already had apartments of their own lived, and even how they furnished their homes. I was excited about decorating an apartment, but I knew I had to be realistic about money when buying furniture.

I began calculating how much money I could save within a given time period. If I saved $70 per week until my birthday, I figured I'd have a decent amount, and I could combine it with any scholarship money I got.

So I set a goal. I decided I wanted to have $7,000 saved by the time I was 21. For the months to come, reaching that goal became one of the main things I thought about. I was set on doing it no matter what. But I had no idea just how much determination it would take for me to reach it and how many obstacles I was going to face. Saving money, it turns out, is not easy.

For one, because I work in a woman's clothing store, I end up buying a lot of the clothes the store sells. Sometimes I literally work to pay my layaway bills. Besides the store I work in, there are many other clothing stores in that area. I found myself spending a lot of my hard-earned money on clothes I didn't really need. As reality set in, I told myself, "That's it, I have to stop spending on things like clothes." It wasn't easy and I didn't stop completely, but I did slow down a lot.

*Many times I wanted to quit my job, but that's not how the real world runs. I knew I needed to save money.*

I started college, and started learning just how hard it is to work and go to school. I still had my regular job, but now I had also been given a work study placement at school, which I took advantage of. Work study let me work on my college campus. So I worked between classes, then went to my regular job after school. I was busy…and tired.

hen a blessing came my way. I got financial aid, which helps students pay for college and which really started me on the road to saving. When you get financial aid, it first pays for your tuition, and whatever money is left over goes to you.

After tuition, $3,200 of my financial aid package was left over. I got $1,400 of it my first semester in school and would get the second part the next semester. Some of that money I spent on books and school things. But since I was living in a foster home and not paying for rent or food, I also saved some of it. Instead of spending it all on new clothes (which I was tempted to do), I actually put it away for my birthday, emancipation day. I put it in the bank, along with another $1,400 scholarship I got, plus $560 I'd gotten back from my former foster mother. Things were looking up.

And then things looked down again. I didn't squander my money, I just gave too much of it to people who needed it more than I did. If someone I knew was in need, I just gave them money. I felt like since I had money saved up, I needed to help those close to me. I temporarily forgot that the day would come when I'd really need that money to fall back on. During this time, I went from having $3,800 to only $1,400.

I realized, once again, that I had lost control and had to do something about it. When I started a paid internship, I was determined to save some of the money I'd make there for when I'd age out. I also knew that I would be getting more money back from school financial aid the next semester, so I felt like I was back on my feet again. I reshaped my budget plan. Now it looked like this:

$3,200—financial aid all together (total for both semesters)

$1,400—work

$450—previous savings

$700—internship

$750—discharge grant (money I'd get from my foster care agency when I aged out)

This gave me a total of $6,500—still short $500 if I wanted to reach my goal of $7,000. And already I'd spent about half of my financial aid money on school supplies, clothes, and giving to others. I wondered how I would ever reach my goal.

I figured out different plans, like working more hours at Dress Barn or becoming a lifeguard as well. (I'm a good swimmer and lifeguarding usually pays pretty well.) In the end, I got offered a better, higher-paying internship doing community planning.

Meanwhile, the last year before D-Day progressed, I knew I'd need somewhere to live. I had a friend who owned a house with a basement to rent for $780 per month (this was pretty cheap for the area). She wanted to rent it to me, and I decided to take her up on her offer. I would be living alone, and I like my own space. I can do whatever I want to do and no one can say anything about it.

Of course, there's a flip side to this. There are bills, bills, and more bills, which will be my responsibility alone. But I still want to have my own place—with my own furniture. After I decided to rent the apartment, I started walking from one end of New York to the other, comparing prices on furniture. I wanted a decent bedroom set that would last and a desk where I could study, but as always, I wanted to be careful about money. I also went to see my apartment and decided it will need some cleaning, painting, and decorating when I move in.

Right now I'm getting excited about my new life outside of the system, but also nervous. For the next three months I'm going to concentrate on saving more money. I want to have at least four months' rent put aside to use in case of emergency and I'm close to reaching that goal.

---

*Giselle successfully made the transition from living in foster care to living on her own. She later graduated from John Jay College of Criminal Justice and got a job in social services.*

# Credits

**The stories in this book originally appeared in the following Youth Communication publications:**

"Don't Follow the Leader" (was "Following the Leader") by Anonymous, *Represent*, March/April 2006; "Equal Work, Unequal Pay" by Mitzi Sanchez, *New Youth Connections*, May/June 2011; "The Rags to Riches Myth," by Marco Salazar, *New Youth Connections*, April 2010; "A Dysfunctional Love Story," by Jan Nicole Garcia, *New Youth Connections*, April 2010; "Getting by on Crayon Money," by Diana Moreno, *New Youth Connections*, January/February 1999; "In This Game, The Rich Get Richer," by Melissa Oliver, *New Youth Connections*, September 1997; "Movin' On Up," by Hattie Rice, *New Youth Connections*, December 2005; "Job-Hopping to a Career" by Samantha Flowers, *Represent*, Summer 2012; A Bad Deal," by Anonymous, *Represent*, January/February 2008; "I Took a Scam Job" by Jianxin Shi, *Represent*, Fall 2013; "Job-Hunting Tips," by Shaniqua Sockwell, *Represent*, January/February 1996; "Dream Job or Scam?" by Danielle Chambers, *Represent*, Fall 2010; "Chimore Plus Eight" by Chimore Mack, *Represent*, Fall 2013; "I Keep My Money in the Bank," by Jarel Melendez (was "I Keep My Bling in the Bank," *Represent*, November/December 2005; "A Guide to Drama-Free Banking," by Chantal Hylton, *New Youth Connections*, April 2010;

"My Credit Card Gave Me False Security" by Zhanna Raymond, *Represent*, Fall 2013; "Learning What 'Overdraft' Means the Hard Way" (was "My Green Debit Card") by Chimore Mack, *Represent*, Fall 2010; "We Don't Save It for a Rainy Day" by Natalie Neptune, *New Youth Connections*, November 1997; "Saving Money Makes Me Feel Safe" (was "I'm a Saver") by Damaris Medina, *Represent*, Fall 2010; "I Shopped Until I Dropped...Into Credit Card Debt" (was "Maxed Out") by Xavier Reyes, *Represent*, July/August 2001; "How I Learned to Be Stingy" by Asia Fillmore, *Represent*, Fall 2010; "The Basics of Account-Ability," by Darnise Gilbert, *Represent*, November/December 2005; "Secondhand, First-Rate," by Anita Ames, *New Youth Connections*, April 2009; "Swap and Save," by Anita Ames, *New Youth Connections*, April 2009; ""How Am I Supposed to Pay for College" by Maria Alashola, *Represent*, Fall 2013; "Scam U.: For-Profit Colleges May Rip You Off" by Marco Salazar, *YCteen*, September/October 2011; "Take Charge of Your College Bills," by Marci Bayer, *New Youth Connections*, September/October 2008; "On My Own: An Aging Out Story" by Anonymous, *Represent*, Fall 2013; "Countdown to Independence," by Giselle John, *Represent*, September/October 2004.

# About
# Youth Communication

Youth Communication, founded in 1980, helps teens strengthen the social, emotional, and literacy skills that contribute to success in school, work, and life. We do that by providing educators with uniquely compelling teen-written stories, supported by lessons and professional development. For more information about our stories and programs, go to youthcomm.org.

# About The Editors

**Virginia Vitzthum** is the editor of *Represent*, Youth Communication's magazine by and for youth in foster care. She has written for publications including *Elle*, the *Village Voice*, washingtonpost.com, AlterNet.org, *Time Out New York*, *Ms.*, and salon.com, where she was a columnist. She is the author of a book about Internet dating, *I Love You, Let's Meet*, and a contributor to *Beautiful Trouble*, a book about creative activism. She was managing editor of a book series on substance abuse treatment and has edited many other publications. She has worked at Youth Communication since 2008 and also edited Youth Communication's books on drugs, disabilities, sexuality, and other topics.

---

**Keith Hefner** co-founded Youth Communication in 1980 and has directed it ever since. He is the recipient of the Luther P. Jackson Education Award from the New York Association of Black Journalists and a MacArthur Fellowship. He was also a Revson Fellow at Columbia University.

# More Helpful Resources
# From Youth Communication

 *The Struggle to Be Strong: True Stories by Teens About Overcoming Tough Times.* Foreword by Veronica Chambers. Help young people identify and build resilience with 30 personal stories and lessons. (Free Spirit)

*Real Stories, Real Teens.* Inspire teens to read and recognize their strengths with 26 true stories by teens and lessons. The young writers describe how they overcame significant challenges and stayed true to themselves. Also includes the first chapters from three novels in the Bluford Series. (Youth Communication)

 *Real Jobs, Real Stories.* Teens describe how they got jobs, how they kept them, and what they learned. The lessons help teens learn how to manage the money they earn and how to plan for the future. (Youth Communication)

*The Courage to Be Yourself: True Stories by Teens About Cliques, Conflicts, and Overcoming Peer Pressure.* In 26 first-person stories, teens write about their lives with searing honesty. These stories and lessons will inspire young readers to reflect on their own lives, work through their problems, and help them discover who they really are. (Free Spirit)

 *Real Men: Urban Teens Write About How to Be a Man.* These lessons and true stories by young men that show how they have overcome challenges like peer pressure, absent fathers, anger, and school failure. (Youth Communication)

*Managing Transitions for Teens.* This program is designed to help youth—especially those who've already lived with loss and upheaval—deal with change. The lessons teach teens about the stages of transition and the tools they can use to cope. (Youth Communication)

## Anthologies

*Out With It: Gay and Straight Teens Write About Homosexuality.* Break stereotypes and provide support with this unflinching look at gay life from a teen's perspective. With a focus on urban youth, this book also includes several heterosexual teens' transformative experiences with gay peers. (Youth Communication)

*Things Get Hectic: Teens Write About the Violence That Surrounds Them.* Violence is commonplace in many teens' lives, be it bullying, gangs, dating, or family relationships. Hear the experiences of victims, perpetrators, and witnesses through more than 50 real-world stories. (Youth Communication)

*From Dropout to Achiever.* Young people themselves show how they overcame challenges that stood in the way of graduating or getting a GED, including taking more responsibility, learning to get along with peers, rejecting negative messages from family and peers, and pursuing the goal of college. (Youth Communication)

*Starting With "I": Personal Stories by Teenagers.* "Who am I and who do I want to become?" Thirty-five stories examine this question through the lens of race, ethnicity, gender, sexuality, family, and more. Increase  this book's value with the free Teacher's Guide, available from youthcomm.org. (Youth Communication)

---

*To order these and other books, go to:*
**youthcomm.org**
*or call 212-279-0708 x115*

CPSIA information can be obtained
at www.ICGtesting.com
Printed in the USA
FFOW01n1148031215
19032FF